DATE DUE

DATE DUE		
APR 15 '89		
MAY 16 '89		
DEC 19 '90		

D1266806

NEVER

MARRIED

WOMEN

IN THE SERIES

WOMEN IN THE POLITICAL ECONOMY,

EDITED BY RONNIE J. STEINBERG

Never Married
WOMEN

Barbara Levy Simon

TEMPLE UNIVERSITY PRESS   Philadelphia

Temple University Press, Philadelphia 19122
Copyright © 1987 by Temple University. All rights reserved
Published 1987
Printed in the United States of America

The paper used in this publication meets the minimum
requirements of American National Standard for Information
Sciences—Permanence of Paper for Printed Library Materials,
ANSI Z39.48-1984

Library of Congress Cataloging-in-Publication Data

Simon, Barbara Levy, 1949–
Never married women.

(Women in the political economy)
Includes index.
1. Single women—Pennsylvania—Philadelphia—
Psychology. 2. Aged women—Pennsylvania—Philadelphia—
Psychology. I. Title. II. Series.
HQ800.2.S55 1987   305.4'890652'0974811   87-6457
ISBN 0-87722-497-8 (alk. paper)

For Paula

Contents

Preface

Never Married Women explores the lives of 50 women who have in common an uncommon marital status. I have written this book about them because I want others to learn, as I have, about the diversity of their experiences and perspectives. It is only by immersion in this variety that one can begin to comprehend the discrepancy between popular images of "old maids" and the actualities of single women's daily lives.

I have also written this book because I think that minority groups in any culture occupy a vantage point that permits them, indeed, requires them, to inspect dominant norms and expectations with particular acuity. These 50 women serve as important informants not only about their own lives, but also about the general socialization of women in the United States in their age groups, from sixty-six to one hundred and one years old. Because all the women are now in partial or full retirement, they are able to offer insights about many parts of the life cycle and about the transitions between those parts. They are also able to teach us about subcultural variations in the treatment of women since they come from a range of ethnic and religious groups. Their long employment histories and many decades of relations with families and friends constitute a particularly rich source of information about work, kinship, and intimacy across time.

Unprecedented numbers and proportions of women in the United States in the 1980s are delaying marriage until their mid and late thirties. Many demographers predict that the percentage of American women now between the ages of twenty and forty-five who will remain single throughout their lives will far exceed the rates of never-married women recorded at any time during the past century. Given these changing patterns and projections, we should do well to turn to the reflections of women who have lived among us for at least six decades as single women in a society that expected its women to marry and bear children.

Though women who have never married have often been judged, they have seldom been studied. This book is an early contribution to a wider inquiry that, I hope, will expand exponentially over the next few decades.

Acknowledgments

In preparing this study, my chief debt is to the 50 women who so willingly discussed their pasts and presents with me. Their generosity and curiosity make this book possible. So does their courage.

I thank, also, three teachers. Professor Alice Rossi's dual passions for feminist political action and interdisciplinary women's studies during her years of teaching and writing at Goucher College demonstrated that the scholarship of an activist and the activism of a scholar can be equally and concomitantly distinguished. Professor Jean Baker's devotion to understanding the nineteenth century on its own changing terms taught me to approach the twentieth century in the same manner. Professor Carole Joffe initiated me into the craft of qualitative research while I was a doctoral student at Bryn Mawr College. Her intellectual influence has informed my work from conception to completion.

Crucial financial support for this research came from a National Endowment for the Humanities Summer Seminar Fellowship, a La Salle University Summer Research Grant, a National Institute on Aging Small Grant (#RO3 AGO4694-01,1984), and a New York

State/United Universities Professions New Faculty Development Award in 1985.

The La Salle University Women's Studies Steering Committee of 1979–1984 gave me the quality of intellectual and emotional support that one dreams of, but rarely finds. The Women's Studies Committee's Chairperson, Professor Caryn Musil, now Director of the National Women's Studies Association, was more mentor than colleague in my first five years of teaching. The collegiality of the other members of the Women's Studies Committee, Professors Arleen Dallery, Barbara Millard, Judith Newton, Laura Otten, and Minna Weinstein (the latter now of the Middle States Association/Commission on Higher Education) was also indispensable to me. My colleagues in the Sociology Department at La Salle, in Philadelphia, among them Professors Dennis Brunn, John F. Connors, Finn Hornum, Sybil Montgomery, and Steve Stevenson, were a steady source of help throughout my years at the university.

At the State University of New York at Stony Brook School of Social Welfare, I received indispensable encouragement and criticism from Professors Marcia Abramson, Kathryn Moss, and Stephen Rose. Professors Harvey Farberman, Robert Lefferts, and Elinor Polansky made conceptual and methodological suggestions that proved immediately useful. Dean Ruth Brandwein fostered my writing throughout the two years I taught at Stony Brook.

My new colleagues at the Columbia University School of Social Work have assisted me in completing this work by inviting me into a setting where the intellectual intensity and scholarly productivity are astonishing. I am proud to have joined them.

The reference librarians and collections at Bryn Mawr College, La Salle University, the Health Sciences Library at the State University of New York at Stony Brook, Sarah Lawrence College, Barnard College, and the Columbia University Social Work Library were essential to the research process. The staff at Temple University

Press, Editor-in-Chief Michael Ames and Production Editor Mary Capouya, have helped me transform a private manuscript into a book fit for the public.

Like the fifty women I studied, I have been sustained both by members of my family and by friends during my work on this book. Foremost among them is my mother, Harriet Simon, in whose footsteps I follow as a teacher. My friends have been equally important. Katherine Kurtz's enthusiasm and early contributions were of great significance to me. Azi Ellowitch, Lynne Lamstein, Susan Landau, Anne Lown, and Chris Wing helped, each in her own way, in the shaping of this work. Doren Slade's faith in me has proved invaluable. Jonathan and Tracy Stanton's eagerness to hold this book in their hands helped me make that happen. Above all, I have relied on Paula Hooper Mayhew's devotion to scholarship, women's studies, and me.

NEVER

MARRIED

WOMEN

ONE / Being Marginal: The Single Woman as Caricature

How dare I fail to marry? How peculiar. How brazen. How sad. Or so many believe. Were I weak in the knees, I might believe that too. But, fortunately, my knees are steady and hold me up fine when people give me those patronizing looks and commiserating tones.

As an eighty-two-year old, it's easy to ignore the labels attached to those of us who stayed single. It used to be harder. For example, when I was about forty, my boss asked me out of the blue if I was still in love with my father. By then, I knew enough to make jokes about such foolishness. The only alternative to humor that I could think of was committing mayhem or worse. And how could I explain to the judge that I killed my boss because he saw me as a silly spinster? [July 1983]

2 / Being Marginal

In Anglo-American culture, the never-married old woman is a stock character, a bundle of negative personal characteristics, and a metaphor for barrenness, ugliness, and death. Her obvious undesirability forms the basis for the children's card game, "Old Maids," in which each player tries to avoid coming to the end of the round with the "Old Maid" card in his or her hand. In a phrase, to "get stuck with the Old Maid" is to lose the game.

This view of the never-married woman as an unwanted leftover has inspired more than a parlor game. Such an image enjoys a long history in our language and literature. It stretches from the "spinster" of the fourteenth century, as evidenced by the word itself, which is still used in law for a woman who has never married, through an undeniably rich and varied series of characterizations in fiction and poetry. William Wordsworth bemoaned "maidens withering on the stalk"; William Blake called prudence "a rich, ugly old maid, courted by Incapacity." Alexander Pope caught the image in a couplet: "My soul abhors the tasteless dry embrace/Of a stale virgin with a winter face."[1] More contemporary writers extend the theme. William Faulkner writes: "He was as crochety about his julep as an old maid, measuring everything by a recipe in his head."[2] In order to belittle a man, one need only liken him to an old, never-married woman. Nor are women writers exempt from these prejudices. The novels of Barbara Pym, for example, teem

---

Quotations are taken from interviews I conducted with never-married women, aged sixty-six and older, in the Philadelphia and New York City areas between 1982 and 1984. The bracketed information specifies the date of the interview in which the quoted comment was made. The names of all those interviewed are changed or omitted to ensure confidentiality.

with highly idiosyncratic single women in middle and old age who have many of the negative characteristics of the "old maid."

Not just a literary tradition, this stereotype permeated nineteenth-century British popular culture, rendering the never-married woman "redundant." She fares little better in twentieth-century popular imagery.

The classic image is surprisingly pervasive in everyday life. A contemporary travel guide highlights safety and propriety abroad thus: "Many [streets] are as sedate as your proper maiden aunt." In a popular work on corporate sexism, a female employee characterizes never-married women as people immersed in the trivial: "Women bosses have [this fault, which I call] 'old-maid thinking.' It is eternally thinking in terms of details, not in terms of the big thing—more interested in the details of the means than in the general significance of the results."[3] "Old-maid thinking," to the Sunoco Corporation, entails penny pinching. The never-married old woman in Sunoco's 1983 ad exclaims, "I think it's a sin to waste money, but I want a gas I can rely on!"[4] From eighteenth-century poet to contemporary advertiser, a cultural stereotype remains constant—the notion that a woman who never marries misses out on much of life through prim and peevish parsimony.

Yet, there are important shifts across time in cultural receptivity to female singleness to take note of. Historian Lee Chambers-Schiller documents the expansion of respect for white single women of the middle and upper classes and the broadened social role that they carved out for themselves in the United States between 1810 and 1860. The "Cult of Single Blessedness," as it was called, "upheld the single life as both a socially and personally valuable state" and "offered a positive vision of singlehood rooted in Protestant religion and the concepts of woman's particular nature and special sphere."[5] By the time the women interviewed for this book were born, however, a deviant and despised status for never-married women had reemerged.

When I took the single path—the road less traveled—
few girls were doing so. Back in the 1930s, when I
reached age thirty, I didn't know one single girl my
age but me in my hometown who wasn't married by
thirty. I remember well since my mother taunted me
just about daily with that fact. She would say to me:
"Mary, you're the only girl in the county without a husband. I warned you that that would be sure to happen
if you act so damn proud all the time. Men don't
like that in a woman."

The picture is different now. Single girls are much
more numerous than in my day. Their lot is less peculiar, less subject to scrutiny. I wish I could lead the
single life all over again, this time starting in 1950
rather than in 1905. The underbrush is cleared away
now; people's eyebrows arch less at the sight of a single
woman. I don't mean to say that it would be easy now. I
mean to say that I walked past marriage when that
wasn't done. In the 1980s, it *is* done and done by lots of
them.   [July 1984]

This woman derives the same finding from her impressionistic
observations that some social scientists report: A significantly
higher proportion of women in the United States is forgoing marriage in the 1980s than at any time in the past hundred years.
Twenty-two percent of college-educated women in the United
States born in the mid-1950s will never marry, compared with 9
percent of college-educated women born in the mid-1930s.[6]

This projection has even inspired a *People* magazine cover story.
Four contemporary celebrities who embody male norms of wom-
anly beauty and sexiness grace the cover of the magazine with the
rhetorical question, "Are these old maids?" The text begins,

Spinster. The word conjures up a vivid image in the mind's eye—that of a sharp-tongued, gray-haired lady who is wizened and alone. No children to visit on Thanksgiving. No grandkids to knit booties for. No kindly gent with whom to share those sunset years.[7]

Why are higher percentages of American women remaining single than in the past? Increased female participation in the labor market produces a higher proportion of women who are financially independent, though often that independence is of the economically marginal variety. Increased availability, acceptance, and usage of contraception and abortion make heterosexual intimacy without marriage more likely. These material forces, together with the cultural impact of feminism and of the gay rights movement, open more widely to women the door to single lives of dignity, choice, and meaning.

Nonetheless, many women still seek marriage. For these women, however, an imbalance in the ratio of available unmarried women to unmarried men in their thirties and forties results in a scarcity of marriageable men.[8] This unavailability of eligible men is particularly exaggerated for women who deferred marriage while pursuing their education and careers. They encounter a cultural lag between genders. Educated women who want to marry prefer men with equivalent or superior training and education as mates. However, "the cultural pattern is still for men to choose women who are not their equals."[9]

The projected rising tide of never marrying among contemporary women in the United States heightens the importance of investigating the experience of women who chose single life at much earlier points in this century. The autobiographical reflections in this book provide long-neglected insights about the symbolic and material worlds of never-married old women. They offer a view from the edge of twentieth-century patriarchy and capitalism, and they reveal much about the processes of domination and marginalization of subject groups in general.

A major contribution that old, single women offer, the firsthand accounts of their daily lives, is a necessary corrective for the distorted images of single women perpetuated by both popular and "high" culture. These self-descriptions (together with interpretations of them) constitute the major focus of this book. Indeed, this study was guided throughout by Clifford Geertz's counsel that the most fitting task of social science is to search for the meanings people ascribe to their own existences, to interpret the "webs of significance" humans have themselves "spun" and in which they are "suspended."[10]

The 50 women whom I interviewed for this study were born between 1884 and 1918, and come from diverse ethnic, religious, and social-class backgrounds. The qualitative records they put forth counter the reductive portrayals of single women that still predominate.

> Nothing is more ridiculous than someone who says, upon learning that I never got married, "Oh, you would like my Aunt _____! She never got married either. You two would have a lot in common."
>
> That sort of comment gives me some idea of what a black person feels like when whites assume that he either knows or would like to know any other black person who happens to be in the vicinity. Common skin color a friendship makes? Common marital status a friendship makes? Wrong in both cases.
>
> Some single women I meet are pearls to be treasured. Others are just plain boring. Some are not to be endured. The fact is that, like married women, single women come in all flavors and styles. [August 1984]

The stories and reflections of the never-married women recorded here replace oversimplification with nuance and substitute first-person observation for presupposition. These women also throw light on the "pushes and pulls" toward both singleness and marriage that Peter Stein has identified.[11]

Another major present that never-married women offer is a view of patriarchal capitalism from its unmarried margins. They discuss in intimate detail the privileged statuses of marriage and of men. Their stories are, in Peter Stein's terms, "a testament to the imperialism of marriage . . . for as singles they are still . . . regarded as a residual category."[12]

For black women who had been raised in poor or working-class families, the twin imperatives of getting out of poverty and of evading white men's sexual demands far outstripped the importance of getting married as familial and cultural commands. Early in their lives, these women understood the intersecting racial and sexual caste systems that required them to sell their labor in dirty work at low pay, in domestic or farm work. They knew firsthand the systematic exclusion of black women from factory jobs, office clerical work, and retail sales positions, which Jacqueline Jones has documented.[13] They also had personal knowledge of the prevalence of rape and sexual harassment of black women by white men. The cultural message given the 12 black women whom I interviewed by their families and communities was to study, work, and pray their way out of economic misery and sexual vulnerability. Most of these 12 women were encouraged to marry, but *not* with the urgency with which they were exhorted to get an education, a steady and respectable job, and to stay close to God. One black women, raised by parents who were tenant farmers, commented:

> About once a day my parents spelled out what I should become. They talked about me studying to be a school-teacher and painted quite a clear picture of the alterna-

tives. If I didn't go to college, I would become a tenant
farmer, starving like they were. Or I would become a
maid who cleaned up after white people's dirt. Or I
would become a "woman of Satan," someone who slept
around and drank cheap bourbon on Sunday mornings.

I don't ever remember my folks worrying about my
getting a husband. That was *way* down the list of what
they cared about. [March 1984]

Elizabeth Higginbotham, in studying the priorities of educated
black women in the contemporary United States, has found discernible class differences in their life preferences. Black women
from established middle-class families were expected both to marry
and to complete college. Those whom she studied from lower
middle-class families were expected, above all, to finish college.
Only then were they encouraged to secure a husband.[14] Emphasizing demographic considerations in black society, Robert Staples has
argued that the severe sex ratio imbalance between black women
and men (in favor of women) has drastically limited the opportunities for black women to marry in twentieth-century America.
As a consequence, a strong demographic pull toward single
status for black women has been created that has not been
felt by white women.[15]

The 5 Hispanic women who were interviewed told a very
different tale. Regardless of the social-class background from
which they came, these women (4 from Puerto Rico and one from
Cuba) spoke of extreme pressure from family, church, and community to marry early and bear children. One of the Puerto
Rican women noted:

The aim of my family from the time my sisters and I
were tiny was to marry us off well. Since my two sisters

did as they were expected, all family eyes began to focus
on me, the oldest sister. My life between ages twenty
and thirty was a story of hints, insults, warnings, and my
mother's tears. The year I turned thirty, they stopped
putting pressure on me. That year they came to see me
as too far gone to redeem. My life got much easier
when the family gave up on me. [February 1983]

All the women, regardless of ethnic background, knew the prevailing stereotypes of never-married women well and the sway such
images had over the thinking of their neighbors, family members,
and colleagues at work. Forty years ago, Everett Hughes captured
the essence of stereotyping as a process when he wrote about the
"master trait or status" assigned to groups and individuals deemed
to be deviant from the dominant culture. In the stereotyping process, one key attribute dominates other attributes in shaping other
people's conception and perception of the holder of that attribute.
This trait is, in Hughes' analysis, formally expected. Along with
the "master trait," a cluster of "auxiliary status traits," or infor-
mally expected characteristics, is attributed to the bearer of the
master trait.[16] If color is the master trait, laziness, dirtiness, loose
morals, and general inferiority are the associated auxiliary traits
attached to white people's view of people of color. If old age is the
master trait, senility, uselessness, and antiquated thinking are a few
of the informal characteristics expected by younger observers.

Old, single women carry with them three master traits—old
age, female gender, and never-married status. When an old, single
woman in our culture is black, Hispanic, or Asian, she bears at
least four master statuses. The same is true for single old women
who are physically disabled. Context, of course, determines which
trait will stand out and elicit stigma that is felt at a particular
moment. Black women may experience their race as their master

trait in white-dominated situations, but among their family members and with black neighbors, the same women may find their marital status to be most salient. A woman with cerebral palsy judged her disability to be her primary sign of abnormality, except on those rare occasions when she was in a group of severely disabled people. Small wonder, then, that these never-married women report that a long, unbecoming list of characteristics has been affixed to them, and that a few of the women (though surprisingly few) internalized the judgments.

What fuels this stereotyping process? Why do dominant groups and individuals and their upwardly mobile allies bother to worry about those on the borders of their group? Anthropologist Mary Douglas seeks an answer to such questions in her studies of taboos, pollution, and cross-cultural categories of undesirability. She concludes that:

> So many ideas about power are based on an idea of society as a series of forms contrasted with nonform. There is power in forms and other power in the inarticulate area, margins, confused lines, and beyond the external boundaries. . . . Where the social system requires people to hold dangerously ambiguous roles, these persons are credited with uncontrolled, unconscious, dangerous disapproved powers.[17]

The very murkiness of marginal people's situation disturbs those in a better-defined position. Douglas suggests words about witches that may well apply to perceptions of never-married old women:

> Witches are social equivalents of beetles and spiders who live in the cracks of the walls and wainscoting.

They attract the fears and dislikes which other ambigui-
ties and contradictions attract in thought structures,
and the kind of powers attributed to them symbolize
their ambiguous, inarticulate status.[18]

Michelle Fine and Adrienne Asch's analysis of disabled women
is highly relevant to the situation of never-married old women.
They argue that disabled women have fewer socially sanctioned
roles than do nondisabled women or disabled men.[19] Such women
are perceived as inadequate or unable to perform the economically
productive roles traditionally ascribed to men. They are also assumed to be unable, by virtue of their disability, to fill the nurturant and reproductive roles of "able" women. Never-married
women are permitted, until old age, the first role, that of economic
productivity—at least minimally. Society, however, does not grant
them a nurturant role in relation to adults or children outside the
family, though, as we shall see, they are heavily relied upon for
nurturance within the family. Such a reduction in roles can lead to
feelings of worthlessness, to taking on a more traditional version of
femininity, or to a high degree of dependence on others and on
external institutions for identity and validation.[20]

The stigma of never-married status in a world of married
couples or formerly married individuals "spoils the identity," in the
words of Erving Goffman, of women who remain single throughout their lives.[21] Once one's identity is spoiled, Goffman speculates,
only three strategies are open to reduce the stigmatization. The
individual can attempt to correct the deviant trait. (She can find a
husband.) Or she can commit much energy to mastering activities
considered, in the ordinary course of things, to be beyond her ken
as an unmarried woman. (She can devote herself to caring for children, personally or professionally; she can make herself as conven-

tionally attractive as possible, through stylish dressing and make-up; or she can "talk up" an actual or fictional history of popularity with men and romantic adventure.) The third strategic choice of the woman with the spoiled identity is to diverge from the mainstream and adopt an unorthodox, indeed radical, interpretation of the nature and value of her identity.[22] (The never-married old woman can proclaim to herself, and the world, the dignity of a chosen single life.) This is Clara Mayo's concept of "positive marginality," and it is, in fact, what many of these 50 very interesting women have done.[23]

All 50 women whom I interviewed were "deviants." In remaining single, they deviated from a powerful cultural norm and an overwhelming demographic pattern, to which 93 to 95 percent of the women in their birth cohorts conformed. Which of Goffman's trinity of strategies did these 50 women use, in the light of such deviancy, to maintain their identities, a project which sociologist Sarah Matthews conceptualizes as a "process of negotiations"?[24] How, in her words, did these 50 "actors mediate those forces" that have labeled and treated them as oddities, that have socially constructed and sustained their marginality?[25]

Some of the women, 8 in number, have fully and uncritically internalized the notion that normal women marry. The women in this group employed the first strategy, trying to become "normal," until they conceived of themselves as too old to marry. All but one of this cluster of 8 then employed the second strategy as a way of adapting to an undesired single role and a judgmental world.

A much more ambivalent orientation toward the deviancy of single status was exhibited by a second subset of 20 women in the group. These women reported that, most of the time, they felt quite clear about their preference for single life. They acknowledged, however, periodic doubts as to whether this clarity and preference was healthy or pathological. Their approach alternated between adopting traditionally "feminine" concerns, postures, and appearances and the more defiant tack of actively ignoring prevailing definitions of acceptability in women. This alternative, of trying to look like "normals," is reminiscent of the approach chosen during the mid-nineteenth century by single women active in reform movements such as antislavery work. These reformers, Chambers-Schiller reports, were especially sensitive to public attitudes concerning the "unnaturalness" of their spinsterhood.[26] They "felt the deviancy of their unmarried state, and often reacted by emphasizing the feminine qualities in their personalities and behavior in ways which limited their contributions to the cause of reform."[27]

Unlike their nineteenth-century predecessors, the never-married women I interviewed risked, by remaining single, "double failure" (a term devised by Suzanne Gordon to express the combination of sexual and emotional demands made on twentieth-century women).[28] Until the writings of the early sexologists and Sigmund Freud began to permeate American culture in the second and third decades of the twentieth century, Victorian and Edwardian notions of womanhood (that is, *respectable* womanhood—the qualifying term bestowed only upon white, middle-class women) prevailed, which assumed female sexual indifference.[29] As a consequence, nineteenth-century single women in America, if they were white and middle class, failed to marry, but they failed no *sexual* test. (Neither did "less than respectable" women of the nineteenth century—those who were women of color from all classes and white women from poor or working-class backgrounds. Such women, in sharp contrast with white, middle-class women, were considered "animalistic" and lustful. These women did not "fail" to be sexual if they did not marry, for their sexual availability and utility were seen to be traits attached to their color or social class, not functions of their marital status.)

By the time most of the women I interviewed hɾd reached adulthood, in the 1920s or 1930s, married women of all class and racial groups in America were understood to be sexual creatures. Therefore, the term "old maid," when applied to a twentieth-century woman, connoted both sexual and marital lacunae. The 20 women who preferred single life, but vacillated in their belief in its legitimacy and normalcy, were acutely aware of their "double failure." Their defensiveness took several forms. They either conformed (strategy 2) early in life and rebelled at some later point, or they oscillated between periods of conformity and periods of rebellion. Some even attempted strategies 2 and 3 at the same time. They *explicitly* rejected the necessity or preferability of married life for women, yet strove to reassure themselves and others of their likeness to married women. One woman captures this duality:

> Marry? Why would I marry? As a single woman, I had my freedom all of the time. Some relatives hinted every now and then that there was something wrong that I had not ever married. But I wasn't odd. I dressed lacier than a lot of married women I saw on my block. I spent more time with my brothers' kids than a lot of my married neighbors spent with their *own* children. And, I can assure you, I had nothing whatsoever to do with women who didn't like men. Why, on my job, I fired one woman the minute I learned that she was, well, you know, like that tennis star. You know, a "lezzie." I have no truck with those sorts. [February 1984]

The third kind of relation to the deviancy of single status cultivated by some of the women I interviewed was outright and sustained rejection of the marital norm. Twenty-two women took that position in early adulthood and held to it without deviating from strategy 3. Some of these 22 women did so defiantly; others maintained their resistance in a more relaxed and insouciant manner. The latter attitude was expressed well by one of them:

Heavens, I have had a nice life! Some thinks I would have had a better time if I'd have married. But I don't see it that way. I've just done the things I've wanted to do, money permitting. If I wanted to travel, I found a way. If I got lonely, I made new friends. If I wanted younguns around, I found some. There was never a big deal about happiness. You either make it for yourself or you don't. It doesn't have much to do with marriage. Now, I would have been just as happy if I had married, for, after all, anybody I would have settled down with would have been fun, I can assure you. You see, I would have made sure of that. And if things had gotten nasty in that marriage, I would have ended the nastiness or ended the marriage. [July 1983]

Resistance to conforming to marital norms and to appearing "normal" took many forms among these 22 women who chose strategy 3 as a way of living. For some, the resistance was expressed in their dress. Five of the women reported that they tried to invent a wardrobe that was neither masculine nor traditionally feminine. Others talked about playing sports in a public and competent way to "remind myself and everyone else," as one woman said, "of how active women can be if given the chance to come out of the cage." Many of the 22 reported that they competed at work for promotions and distinction in order to insist on their "place in the sun," as one woman phrased it. This competitiveness, one example of which follows, was a repeated theme among the "resisters":

> Teddy Roosevelt was my idol because he gave everything his all. I have done the same, especially because lots of people expect "spinsters" to sit on the sidelines and meekly resign themselves to life's crumbs. I decided early that if I was going to be a single woman I was going to do it with flair. So I set my sights on being factory foreman. No woman had done that in the eighty-four years of the factory's existence before I did it. Oh, lots of men on the floor had a lot to say about that. They spread lies and accusations that hurt me. Some suggested that I thought I was a man. Some said I was missing some female hormones. Some called me "butch" whenever they talked to me. My skin got thicker and thicker and so did my paycheck. My pride in myself grew all the while.   [September 1982]

Others resisted conformity through living with or developing deep friendships with other single women. Several of these women remarked on the risks they took in doing so. They knew that if they had lived with relatives or alone they would have been subjected to pity, but not scandal. Upon sharing a household or most of their observable existence with a special single-woman friend, they made themselves vulnerable to suspicions of hoi .osexuality. One woman commented:

> Elsie and I made no bones to anyone about how important we were to each other. We went everywhere together. We bought a house together and shared forty-one years together. Her mother and father begged her to "consider

appearances" and to live with them instead. My boss called me in once to ask me if my pastor approved of my way of living. None of them used the word, but they all worried that we were homosexuals. Elsie and I made a pact early on that we would never take the easy out and give anyone any answers. To this day, neither of us have betrayed that promise. It is simply no one's business. That holds in this interview, by the way. It's none of your business, either. [May 1984]

It is important, before we conclude this discussion of the resistant 22, to make clear that most of these women had intricate friendship, neighborhood, and kin relations with men as well as women, and with children as well as adults. Thirteen of these 22 women chose work that focused on teaching or delivering services to children and their families. How, then, are these links with nuclear families, men, and children different from those I have categorized as conformist behavior within strategy 2? The distinction is one of perceived motivation. Those women from either the cluster who mixed strategies 2 and 3 or from the group who employed only strategy 3, who appeared to have chosen a job or a relationship out of *commitment* to that work or to that person, have *not*, in my judgment, conformed. Those choices of jobs, activities, or companions that seemed to me to be inspired primarily by fear, the fear that they might be considered odd if they did not act in those directions, I have dubbed "conforming behavior." An example of each, which will help make this admittedly subjective distinction clearer, follows:

> From the time I was tiny, I wanted to be a teacher. I loved "playing school" as much as some other kids loved playing hookie. Mostly I wanted to work with

little children, the ones between five and eight, who are finding out about the world. You see, I knew early on that I had a certain gift for making little kids laugh and get pleasure from exploring ideas. Happily, that all turned out to be true. My students came back year in and year out to tell me that I had made school a fine place for them. That is enormously gratifying, you know. [December 1983]

Contrast that obvious confidence and commitment with the following:

Why did I choose teaching, you ask? Well, because I didn't dare do what my heart dictated—become a horse trainer. As a child, I had learned to ride and all about caring for horses. My father, you see, had been a horse trainer for a rich family in Glenside. But when I was graduating from high school, I thought a long time about my prospects. I guessed that I would never marry because I seemed to prefer to be alone than to be with boys. I saw, therefore, that I would have to earn my own keep.

Now, very few women became horse trainers. In fact, I had known one married woman who had trained horses. But the thought of being a single woman who did that seemed like asking for trouble. Why, just think of the things people would have said about an "old maid" who did men's work. I knew myself well enough to know that such slights would do me a lot of damage. So I looked around instead for something to do that nobody would give a second thought to. Teaching was it. [October 1983]

Avoidance of stigma motivated this second teacher to join that profession. In a similar way, fear of being called a "man hater" encouraged another woman to find a man friend:

> The men and girls at the office thought I was out to lunch one day and started to talk about me. They wondered out loud if I was "strange." They said they had never seen me with a man. Somebody said that I liked women too much.
>
> I was depressed for months. Then I met at a family picnic a man who wasn't what you'd call exciting, but who was pleasant enough. I remember thinking at that picnic that it would help me a lot to show up with this fellow at work a few times. So I engineered a "lunch relationship." Over two years, we only saw each other at lunch. But let me tell you, that was enough to bring me back into the zone of the acceptable. I'm not proud, you understand, of using that nice man in that way. But it was important to me to change the way they saw me. [January 1984]

This woman's self-consciousness and instrumental pursuit of acceptability sprang from her awareness, still keen at seventy-nine, of her membership in a tiny statistical minority.

The vast majority of American women born in this country since the seventeenth century, between 89 and 96 percent, have married.[30] The number of never-married women in the colonial period who lived past forty-five and did not marry was very small—only a small percentage of adult women, according to Chambers-Schiller.[31] During the last quarter of the eighteenth century, the proportion of women who remained single began to increase, and this trend continued through the first three-quarters of the nineteenth century. Of those women born between 1835 and 1838, 7.3 percent remained single; between 1845 and 1849, 8.0 percent; and between 1855 and 1859, 8.9 percent. The trend reached its peak among women born between 1865 and 1875, of whom 11 percent did not marry.[32]

The last two decades of the nineteenth century saw a decline in the proportion of women born in those years who never married. Among the birth cohort of the oldest women in this study, those born between 1884 and 1894, 8.7 percent did not marry. An even more dramatic decline in the never-married rate occurred among American women born in the first two decades of the twentieth century. Between 1915 and 1918, the birth-years of the youngest women studied here, only 4.8 percent remained single. In short, during the forty years between 1875 and 1915 the percentage of women who did not marry shrank to less than half the proportion of those who remained single in 1875.[33]

Singleness among women over thirty-five years old, born between World War I and the U.S. Census of 1980, remained low— 5.5 percent or lower. In 1979, only 5.3 percent of women in the United States thirty-five years old or older had never been married.[34] Clearly, women who did not marry in twentieth-century America constitute a statistical minority. One woman, interviewed at age ninety, commented on this minority status:

At thirty, there still were a few of us "left on the vine." By forty, there was no one but Georgia O'Connor and me without a husband from the sixty-four of us here in St. Margaret's parish who took First Communion together. By forty, I was well-accustomed to being a single "goat" outside the "flock" of married sheep. In fact, I could see by age twenty-five that a single path would be an unusual path for a woman in my situation who did not become a nun. So I had to make up my own rules for living, which I found easy to do. [August 1982]

Others in the group of women interviewed reacted to their minority status in different ways. Some railed against it; some ignored it; and some took pride in it, as the woman quoted above did. Some developed critiques of the majority's mores, and a few made the "marriage imperative" a foundation of their self-definition and self-loathing. This broad range of reactions to membership in a never-married minority was relatively easy to discover since most of the women viewed our interviews as opportunities to talk about those parts of their lives most important to them as well as those elements they deemed most misunderstood by others. A self-selected group by virtue of their consenting to be interviewed by someone explicitly focusing on never-married women, they were unusually receptive to questioning.

I suppose I will let you interview me if you think some good will actually come of it. But don't just write something that will collect dust in some dusty library. Write something that other single women will read. Write something that people who care for us in old age will read. Most of all, tell them why we matter. [September 1983]

Fifty women were interviewed between 1982 and 1984, all of whom never married and were sixty-five or older. Forty-eight of the women lived in the greater Philadelphia area; 2 lived in the New York metropolitan area. The 50 women were chosen to be as representative as possible of racial, social-class, educational, religious, and age variations in the population of women, sixty-five years old and older, who lived in or near Philadelphia in the early 1980s.

The women with whom I spoke were identified by staff people I contacted in senior citizen centers, community centers, churches and synagogues, social service agencies, and community groups. Friends and colleagues from a broad range of occupations and many parts of the Philadelphia area also suggested women to interview. Students at La Salle University, where I was then teaching, proposed other never-married women for interviewing. To supplement these suggestions, I placed notices in selected urban and suburban neighborhood newspapers. In addition, the women interviewed were asked for likely prospects among their neighbors and acquaintances. The composition of the final pool of 50 women is outlined in Table 1.

How does this group of 50 never-married women compare with a national pool of American men and women sixty-five years old and older at the time of the 1980 U.S. Census? Racially, the group has a somewhat larger proportion of black, Hispanic, Asian, and Native American residents than overall U.S. percentages of senior citizens in 1980.[35] I purposefully included slightly larger proportions of minority women for two reasons: to reflect the higher proportions of minority residents in East Coast metropolitan areas than in the nation as a whole and to ensure the inclusion of perspectives too rarely solicited and too often presumed to be identical or similar to those of white women.

Occupationally, this group has a disproportionately high number of professional women—34 percent of the whole, compared with the 10.3 percent of U.S. women sixty-five years old and older in 1983 who were professionals.[36] A smaller proportion of this pool of women, 4 percent, worked in sales than in the general population of women sixty-five and older in 1983.[37]

In each racial group and overall, the 50 women in this sample were *much* better educated than the national pool of all women in

TABLE 1 / Characteristics of Women Interviewed, 1982–84

Characteristic	Number
Race	
White	30
Black	12
Hispanic	5
Asian	2
Native American	1
Age at interview	
65–69	7
70–74	11
75–79	18
80–84	8
85–89	2
90–94	1
95–99	1
100–105	2
Occupation	
Domestic worker	6
Factory worker	8
Retail sales	2
Clerical worker	13
Lab technician	1
Professional	17
Managerial	3
Education	
2nd grade	3
6th grade	2
8th grade	5
10th grade	3
High school diploma	11
College, nursing, or normal school	15
Master's degree	6
Ph.D. or equivalent	5

TABLE 1 / *(continued)*

Religion	
Protestant	25
Catholic	17
Jewish	5
Buddhist	1
Agnostic	2
Country of origin	
Native born (incl. 4 from Puerto Rico)	44
Foreign born (1 each from China, Cuba, Germany, Italy, Jamaica, Russia)	6
Residence during most of adult life	
Rural	2
Suburban	21
Urban	27
Residence at time of interview	
Own home	16
Own apartment	16
Relative or friend's home	2
Boarding house	1
Retirement community	15
Nursing home	0
Living arrangement at time of interview	
Alone	4
With friend(s)	15
With family member(s)	31

the United States in their age group. As of 1981, 50 percent of all women sixty-five years old and older had completed twelve years or more of schooling. Only 6.8 percent of all women in the United

States sixty-five years or older in 1981 had completed college.[38] By comparison, 74 percent of this sample had completed twelfth grade or more: 22 percent had finished high school; 30 percent had completed college, nursing school, or normal school; 12 percent had obtained a master's degree; and another 10 percent had earned a Ph.D. in social science or the humanities or a doctorate in nursing or social work.

The mean level of education achieved by this group of 50 women, 13.6 years, though relatively high, is somewhat lower than the remarkably high mean educational level of 15.9 years completed by single women nationally in 1977.[39] Single women in this country, on average, obtain many more years of schooling than do their married or formerly married counterparts. This group of 50 never-married women is no exception to that pattern.

The religious identification of these women was similar in most respects to the country's pool of women who were sixty-five and older in 1984.[40] An exception is the overrepresentation of Jews among these women: 10 percent of the group was Jewish, though only 4 percent of all U.S. women sixty-five and older were Jewish in 1984.[41] Because Philadelphia has a larger proportion of Jewish residents than the nation as a whole, I intentionally increased the number of Jews in the pool of women I interviewed.

The percentage of foreign-born women in the group, 12 percent, was almost identical to that of the general population of women sixty-five and older in 1980.[42] The preponderance of urban and suburban women in the interviewed group and the tiny percentage of rural residents who do not live within 25 miles of a city of 100,000 people are also reflective of the nation's overall residency pattern in 1980.[43]

The age distribution of this group of women favors the older categories of the elderly. Never-married women sixty-five to sixty-nine years of age are underrepresented here, and those in the seventy-five to seventy-nine-year-old category are overrepresented, as are women in the eighty to eighty-four age group.[44] The majority of women discussed here, 54 percent (27 women), were born between 1900 and 1910; 80 percent (40 women) were born between 1900 and 1915.

None of the 50 women lives in a nursing home. Since I wanted to study how never-married women control their lives and see themselves, I excluded women in these institutions, although never-married women constitute a disproportionately large portion of the nursing-home population. (Never-married women are only 2.8 percent of the adult population over the age of fifty-five, yet constitute 10.2 percent of the nursing-home population in the United States.)[45] Indeed, never-married people in the United States have very high rates of institutionalization, compared with the general population.[46]

To explore the economic, psychological, and social strategies that never-married women have used at different points in their life cycle to construct lives in a world of couples, I conducted and taped in-depth interviews with each of the 50 women. The interviews took place in a setting chosen by the woman who was being interviewed, which was, in all but two instances, her own residence. The time spent in interviewing each woman varied considerably, depending upon her health, endurance, and schedule, but the average interview lasted 5.3 hours, conducted in two sittings.

The foci of the interviews were the woman's reflections on her relationship to her family of origin, her friendships, her work life, her aging and retirement experiences, and her attitudes toward marriage and her own singleness. (Initially, I had intended to investigate each woman's recollection and interpretation of her sexual history, but that topic was dropped when it quickly became apparent that many of the first 15 women interviewed were offended by questions on sex and sexuality and were unwilling to discuss them.

Indeed 11 of the women agreed to be interviewed only on the condition that I not ask any questions about sex.)

The language with which the women in the interviews expressed their opinions and characterized their lives ranges from highly formal to informal and from Victorian to modern, just as the women themselves vary greatly in temperament and style. Some of the direct quotations in this book seem strikingly contemporary in tone; colloquialisms coined in the last fifteen years dot their speech. I attribute this linguistic contemporariness to the notable activeness of many of the women and to their regular engagement with people of diverse age groups. Many mentioned watching the Phil Donahue Show on television and other talk shows, another possible influence on their usage. Some of the women, upon reviewing transcriptions of their interviews, were surprised to discover so much contemporary slang in their speech. Not one of the women, it is interesting to note, sought to reword her response.

The stories in this book and their interpretations comment on the ongoing tension between the received and the experienced meanings of never-married existence among women. This commentary discloses and reveals, in 50 versions, both the discrepancy and the correspondence between the culture's canonical expectations of singlehood and the lived experience of that condition. The *subjectivity* of these women's reports, in short, is important.

In exploring this subjectivity, one must proceed with care since retrospective interpretation that aims to explore, in a nonjudgmental manner, the meaning of a socially devalued identity to its bearers, may, unwittingly, strain so hard to avoid reinforcing existing stigma that devaluation is transformed into its opposite, an overestimation of the identity under study. In this case, an attempt to understand the significance of singleness to a group of single women may encourage both the researcher and the women to *overvalue* the salience of never-marriage and to exaggerate the underlying agency and the merits of being single. I have kept this danger in mind throughout these investigations and, I hope, my conscious effort has minimized the risk.

What follows is a portrait of 50 rebels. As women brought up in a society and period that taught them to marry and bear children, they flouted this central cultural rule. They disobeyed patriarchal preference and consequently, as we shall see, they have endured the economic hardships and social stigma that women without men face. They have swum upstream, having selected their own stroke and pace. Most have done so with enthusiasm and self-respect that give the lie to all-too-familiar stereotypes.

T WO / Being Single

They are not halves, needing complements, as are the masses of women; but evenly balanced well rounded characters; therefore are they models to be reached by the average women we everyday meet.

—SUSAN B. ANTHONY, 1877[1]

Clifford Geertz, a leading scholar/explorer of peoples and cultures different from his own, has set as a goal for himself and his discipline of anthropology the determination of "how . . . people . . . define themselves as persons, [and] what goes into the idea they have . . . of what a self . . . is." He proposes not only an aim but also a method with which to achieve a faithful understanding of individuals' conceptions of themselves and of what it means to be a person in a particular culture and time. Geertz obtains this "local knowledge" of informants' notions of themselves and of selfhood by alternating between two perspectives: one derived from immersion in the intimate daily details of informants' actions, thoughts, feelings, and imaginings; the other drawn from synoptic generalizations that a trained observer makes in contextualizing and interpreting the meaning and significance of informants' definitions of reality.[2] The former spotlights the *minutiae* of impressions that actors themselves identify as salient; the latter attends to the *contours* of meaning of a given people or individual, identified through comparison, contrast, and overview by an empathic outsider.

To make the method of discerning a "local knowledge" of people's definitions of selfhood more explicit, Geertz borrows two concepts from psychoanalyst Heinz Kohut, who made a distinction between "experience-near" and "experience-distant" concepts. Experience-near concepts are those that a patient or informant uses easily, indeed effortlessly, in defining her or his feelings, thoughts, hopes, and fears. Experience-distant concepts, by contrast, are those that specialists or theorists have developed in the process of analyzing the overarching characteristics of an individual, a group, a phenomenon, or a subculture. For example, "fear and hunger" felt by a welfare mother responsible for three children is a far more "experience-near" concept than the "feminization of poverty." Or the "love" an adolescent student feels for a teacher is experience-near, compared with the concept of "identifying a role model." Geertz suggests that a researcher's mission is "to grasp concepts that, for another people, are experience-near, and to do so well enough to place them in illuminating connection with experience-distant concepts theorists have fashioned to capture the general features of social life."[3] This chapter attempts to interweave the insights gained in both the near and distant approaches to understanding the lives and views of 50 single women born in the United States between 1884 and 1918.

> The woman who will not be *ruled* must live without marriage.
> —SUSAN B. ANTHONY, 1877[4]

Many of the women I interviewed (34 of 50) initiated comments that sounded this same note. In many different words and with varying emphases, these women stressed the importance of autonomy in their existence. Some saw in the institution of marriage chiefly the subordination that accompanies the "wifely role":

> Men? Men have been important to me all my life. I have had friendships and love and sex with men since I was a young thing in Detroit before what we used to call the "Great War." Long relationships and short ones, they have kept me alive and kicking. Why, Joe and I dated every Wednesday and Saturday from 1959, when his wife passed away, until two years ago, when Joe's stroke took his mind away. How I miss those evenings!
>
> You see, dear, it's *marriage* I avoid, not men. Why would I ever want to be a wife? People expect you to be

under your husband's thumb or to be his good right arm when you get married, regardless of what you or he wants. Who needs that load on their shoulders when life is hard enough already? A wife is someone's servant. A woman is someone's friend. [July 1983]

Others specifically valued freedom from a husband's rule. One woman expressed this vigorously:

The closer we got to the wedding day, the more Peter began to act like a bully. He had cooked for himself for nine years. All of a sudden, when we got engaged, he wanted me to do all the cooking. In public places, he started to act like my boss. Now, one boss, the one I had at work at the time, was enough for me. So I told him: "Look, Pete, let's call this off and just be friends. This marriage stuff is just getting in our way." That's what we did. We stayed close for a few years, but then he told me he wanted a "real wife," one who would know that a man should "wear the pants" in a relationship. He actually used those words! Believe me, I urged him to find that sort of woman for himself, because I *wasn't* it. [August 1984]

Many were concerned about maintaining their autonomy in relation to the families from which they sprang. Despite the deep loyalty to kin of most of the women, which will be explored in detail later, they nonetheless made a clear distinction between being committed to one's family and being "swallowed up" by it. A black woman, born in 1896, presented her concerns about autonomy, in relation to both her family of origin and a family she might help construct, in her own terms:

> My momma was a slave in South Carolina, so I know about what that word means. I never wanted to be anyone's slave, not a white man's and not a black man's. I didn't marry because that looked dangerously close to slavery to me. Neither did I let my father or sisters push me around after I was a full grown woman. They wanted me to fetch and be there for them a lot because I was the only one not married. I took the bull by the horns, though. I told them I would be glad to help them out a lot, but that they should not take me for granted. I told them I would have to see each time if I could give the kind of help they wanted. You see, I won't be anyone's "nigger," not my boss's, not my poppa's, and not some other man's, just because he stood in front of an altar with me one Sunday morning when we were still too stuck on each other to know better. [April 1984]

The concept of independence, then, pervades the self-portraits the women draw. Their emphatic refusal to be "yoked by wifing," as one woman expressed it, is paralleled by their resistance to viewing themselves as part of a group of never-married women. Over and over again, they discouraged any discussion of the common ground they share with other women of their age and marital status. They were imbibers of the American potion of individualism and distanced themselves from identification with a devalued social category.

This unwillingness to identify with a culture of single women stands in sharp contrast to a central finding of Martha Vicinus's study of unmarried women born in the 1840s, 1850s, 1870s, and 1880s in Britain. These women of earlier generations created, with great enthusiasm, what Vicinus terms a "richly nurturing [single] women's subculture" in the schools, colleges, religious orders, professions, settlement houses, and political organizations they created. By the time that most of the women whom I interviewed were approaching adulthood, in the 1920s and 1930s, they may have found such communities of single women in the American context less than appealing because of those institutions' financial vulnerability, reputations contaminated by Freudian suspicions of homosexuality, and outdated ideology of essentialism that proclaimed the inherent moral superiority of women and the preferability of women's separate spheres.[5]

The 50 women in my study expressed no interest in being part of a single-woman's caste, nor did they see themselves as members of a special or superior gender or category. For most of this group of twentieth-century never-married women, single status was a chosen status. Yet the choice to remain single (for all but 2 women, who were members of religious orders) was not a function of mission or moral vocation. Rather, the women chose to remain single for the purpose of preserving their independence or out of commitment to careers.

As important as independence was to these women, of equal weight in their lives and conceptions of self was intimacy with family, friends, and neighbors. A consistent theme that surfaced in the interviews was the value that these women placed on sustaining close relations with family members and friends. For many, the role of daughter had been a crucial one until the death of parents. One woman reported:

> I was fiercely independent from the time I was a small
> child. I was constantly getting in trouble at school and

with my folks for going beyond acceptable boundaries. Why, I even fought my way into a management job in the 1920s in an insurance industry that kept women stuck at the levels of clerk and stenographer.

But my fierce loyalty to mama and papa went hand in hand with all that orneriness. If I got a raise, that meant I could buy them something they needed. If one of them got sick, I was the one who got there first. When mama was widowed, we mourned together the loss of that splendid man. Whenever I was dating someone, I made certain that mama knew him well, too. I saw her every day after papa died, except when my work required me to go out of town or when Sam [her long-time companion] and I went on vacation. I miss both mama and papa terribly, even now, forty-odd years later. [November 1983]

Most of the women also saw themselves as pivotal figures in their siblings' families, taking the roles of sister and aunt very seriously. The reflections of one woman were representative of many of the women interviewed:

Nobody knew those kids like I did, except of course their dad and mom, my brother and his wife. Those children minded me as closely as if they'd been my own. And a good thing it was too, because I missed not a trick; I saw their every coming and going. I knew when they lied and when they told the truth. I knew every victory they had and every defeat. They brought their first sweethearts to me. They let me in on their innermost secrets. I was the one they came to when they needed help with a tough decision or a matter of conscience. [March 1982]

Clearly, the identity of these never-married women hinged as much on their sense of being central characters in their family dramas as on their conception of themselves as independent actors. In the next chapter, the varieties and nuances of their commitment to their families will be explored in greater depth.

Yet, as critical as it was to these women to be a loyal daughter, sister, or aunt, it was of equal, if not greater, importance to them to be a good friend. In the portraits these women drew of themselves over time, they placed their connectedness with friends at the very center of their self-conceptions. One woman communicated this key element of identity thus:

> People often say, "If you have your health, you have everything." I would put it differently. I think that if you have friends, you have everything. Now, mind you, I don't sneer at the importance of health. But my life-blood is the friends I've made over eighty-five years. They restore me; they fuel me; they give me a reason for getting out of bed in the morning. That's always been so, ever since I paled around with Susan when we were four. (She's still my good friend, believe it or not. We've both made it to eighty-five together.) If I am a steady friend till I die to the people who have befriended me, I will die satisfied. [January 1984]

This role of friend appeared integral to the women's sense of themselves at all stages of adult life, but particularly during retirement, when paid work had disappeared as an element in daily life and identity construction. Chapter Four will focus on the rich and complex friendship constellations of these 50 women.

The conceptual and experiential tension created by these women's dual desires to be both independent and intimate appears to have taken no discernible toll on them. When asked about the fit or lack thereof between these two dimensions of self, the women generally answered that, early on in life, they had recognized the delicacy of the balance they required between sociality and autonomy. On the whole, the women expressed a highly self-examined understanding of their need to juxtapose closeness to family and friends with separateness. One woman illuminated this juxtaposition of needs:

> Who am I? Am I a "lone ranger," out on the range of life without companionship or help? Sometimes. In fact, often. But, just as often, I am sitting in the lap of family and friendship, drawing on the wisdom, and laughter, and camaraderie that sisters and buddies offer. It seems that I am both people. One of the reasons I never married, despite five reasonable offers, is that I thought it would be much harder in marriage to go back and forth between being that "lone ranger" and being close. [October 1983]

What proportion of these 50 women is, like the "lone ranger" above, single by conscious choice? What proportion is single by default?

> "I do so wonder, Miss Woodhouse, that you should not be married, or going to be married! so charming as you are!"

Emma laughed, and replied, "My being charming, Harriet, is not quite enough to induce me to marry; I must find other people charming—one other person at least. And I am not only, not going to be married, at present, but have very little intention of ever marrying at all."

—*Emma*, JANE AUSTEN[6]

In distinguishing between those of this group who had little intention of marrying and those who had every intention, a "typology of singlehood," proposed by sociologist Peter Stein, proves helpful.[7] He has suggested a four-cell framework for understanding the varieties of single status in contemporary American life, a modified form of which constitutes Table 2.

The 50 never-married women I interviewed fall into Stein's analytic matrix, as shown in Table 3.

Unlike ninety-three to ninety-five percent of their generational counterparts, the large majority of never-married women whom I interviewed (76 percent) *chose* to be single. They were, as E. P. Thompson would phrase it, agents contributing to the making of their own histories.[8] As conscious actors who have weighed the "pushes and pulls" toward and away from marriage, the 38 women who opted for single life did so for a wide range of reasons.[9]

Of course, in working with sensitive topics and retrospective reflections, one has to be alert to possible discrepancies between conscious rationales and unconscious motivations. For example, it is possible that the desire to remain autonomous stated by some of the women interviewed is a mask for underlying fears of intimacy, men, sex, or childbearing. Having kept this caveat constantly in mind while interviewing the 50 women and interpreting their accounts, I conclude that the large majority of them *preferred* single life to married life. These women, who are informed—

TABLE 2 / Varieties of Singlehood
(after Peter Stein)

	Voluntary	Involuntary
Temporary	Never-marrieds and formerly marrieds open to but not looking for marriage	Those actively seeking mates Those who were not interested but are now looking
Stable	Those choosing to be single Those who oppose marriage Members of religious orders	Never-marrieds and formerly marrieds who wanted to marry or remarry, but have not found a mate—and have accepted singleness as probable life status Persons with physical or psychological impairment

as we all are—by unconscious forces, *chose* to never marry. They may not have chosen single life *only* for the reasons they report, but nonetheless, choose they did. They explain their decisions in various ways.

The 2 women who consider themselves open to marriage, but not looking for a husband (the "temporary, voluntary singles"), both noted that they would have been happy to marry if they had met someone interesting enough. Each reported having turned

TABLE 3 / Never-Married Women's Varieties of Singlehood

	Voluntary	*Involuntary*
Temporary	2 Open to but not looking for marriage	0 Actively seeking mates 0 Were not interested in marriage, but now are looking
Stable	30 Chose to be single 4 Oppose marriage (2 on feminist, 1 on anarchist, and 1 on socialist grounds) 2 Members of religious orders (1 Catholic nun, 1 Methodist missionary)	8 Wanted to marry but have not found a mate—and have accepted singleness as probable life status (7 felt they lost suitors because of care-giving commitments to aging parents) 4 With physical or psychological impair-ment (1 with polio, 1 with cerebral palsy, 1 with hemophilia, 1 with epilepsy)

down several suitors who had not "struck enough sparks," as one put it, to merit giving up a single life that each found fulfilling. One of them commented:

> If the right kind of man shows up, I might well marry him, even now, at seventy-two. But why worry about it? I never did before. Guys would ask me to marry every few years, and I would think about those offers very seriously. But none of them inspired me at all. I have had a rich life, a lot of adventure and freedom, a lot of joy on my job. My friends keep me very happy. So when someone asks me to marry him, I think: "What would I lose? What would I gain?" Up to this point, the loss column always looked longer than the win column. But who knows about the future? [March 1984]

These 2 women share with the 30 "stable, voluntary singles" a many-layered appreciation for the benefits of never-married life. They differ from the 30 in that the former appeared to examine each offer of marriage as an authentic opportunity that needed to be considered carefully on its own merit in that particular moment of their lives. The 30, by contrast, seemed so convinced, at least in retrospect, of the preferability of remaining single that they reported no serious deliberation in the face of marriage offers. One woman's remarks are representative:

> I dated four men over the years who wanted me as a wife. They were darlings, each of them. I spent huge amounts of time with them. But I never for a moment considered marrying one. Well, why would I? I had their company and their attention without all the headaches a wife bears. I knew all about birth control from

the time I was a girl, so I didn't worry about getting pregnant outside of marriage. My life as an "old maid" was just too sweet to yield in order to be Mrs. Somebody Or Other. It's true I would have had much more money if I had married. But I got along ok in my own way. I never had much from my job as a stenographer, but it was enough to keep me honest and happy and free as a bird. [February 1983]

These 30 women, like the 2 women discussed above, valued several dimensions of singleness. The theme of freedom (also discussed above), freedom from the demands embedded ir the institution of a wife's role, emerged over and over again in the interviews as a major reason to remain single. Those 30 women who chose single life did so in part to sustain the autonomy they had experienced as children. One woman said:

My parents had made me early into someone with her own mind. They *required* it of me. I don't know of a marriage around that would even tolerate independent thinking and action in a woman, let alone require it of a wife. [May 1982][10]

One form of autonomy, financial independence, was cited by 18 of these 30 women as being of particular importance to them. Some of these women were committed to their work; some were working only to bring home a paycheck. All 18 considered paid work central to individual freedom; all 18 also thought that marriage would have precluded remaining in the paid labor force.

Other considerations also led these 30 women to choose single life during eras in the twentieth century in which almost all other women chose marriage. Devotion to a job or career contributed to the motivation of 26 of the 30 to remain single. Four of those 26 taught in public schools, positions which, until the 1940s, required single marital status of women as a precondition of employment. One woman said:

> The terms of remaining a teacher here in Philadelphia were crystal clear. We had to be single and beyond reproach, morally speaking. Why, my principal told us that we must not entertain men in our own homes without a chaperone, to avoid a "bad reputation." We were expected to notify him immediately if we got engaged, so that he could arrange for our replacement. I didn't know any married women teaching in the district until the Second World War. Then, of course, they got desperate for teachers, since the men went off. After the war, they did not reenact the regulation which required us to resign if we got married.   [November 1983]

Those who worked as social workers, librarians, nurses, secretaries, and office managers described feeling a pressure within themselves to choose between meaningful work and marriage and an external pressure of an informal kind from suitors and bosses to view marriage and paid work as mutually exclusive. As one woman expressed it:

> I loved my job running that office. I did it for twenty-seven years. It wasn't my whole life, certainly, but it was a highly significant portion. They wouldn't have fired me if I had gotten married. But I would have been unable to be a good wife and also do that job. It required nights, weekends, early mornings, and lots of disrupted

plans. I didn't meet men in those days who would have understood my insistence that the job was as important to me as anything else. Now, I know that such men exist. But back then, they were nowhere to be found, at least not in my circles. [April 1983]

Other women assumed that their work commitments would be necessarily diluted or abolished if they married, because they understood marriage and childraising to be closely linked, even synonymous. They saw no social or emotional supports, such as publicly subsidized child care, to call on if they attempted to balance work as a wife and mother with that of an employee. Indeed, until the late 1960s, the pattern of cultural sermons by church leaders, psychologists, physicians, child-development specialists, and journalists in the popular press strongly discouraged married women and mothers from working, unless they were forced to work through divorce, widowhood, or abandonment. With the exception of the periods during World Wars I and II, during which married women were encouraged, for the sake of the war effort, to perform paid labor while continuing with family duties, prevailing wisdom dictated that women who married would give up paid work and that women who were "invested" in careers or in remaining wage earners would forsake marriage. A woman who worked as a social worker for fifty-two years commented:

In 1928, when I started working in child welfare, it was assumed by me and every man and woman I knew that I had to make a choice between career and family. If I wished to commit myself to social work, I could not expect a husband. Certainly, I could not have children and do my work. For one thing, it was believed very deeply that children would suffer badly if their mother went away during the day to work. Why, I carried that message myself to many mothers in my day. We were all aglow in Sigmund Freud back then and worried a lot about damage to children caused by absent mothers.

I certainly did *not* want to be an absent mother. And then, it didn't occur to us to examine what a father could contribute to childraising. Nor did it occur to me that I could marry, work, and abstain from childbearing and raising. That simply wasn't done, except in cases where a couple was physically unable to have children. [November 1982]

Fear of childbirth motivated 2 of the 30 women to choose a single life. Both women, one born in 1887 and the other in 1902, were deeply impressed as young girls by their mothers' tales of hardship while giving birth. Each of these women noted that she had not realized, until she was past childbearing years, the degree to which fear of giving birth had influenced her, unconsciously, to turn down offers of marriage. The older of the two women reflected:

I would get close to men, but only so close. They would ask for my hand. I would stall and stall until they went elsewhere. Then, in my forty-eighth year, I met somebody whom I was willing to spend a life with. He was a psychiatrist in the hospital I was working in at the time. He wanted to marry. I refused, since I wished to remain independent in a financial sense. So we "shacked up" together for twenty-six years.

I asked myself a lot of times while living with him why I had been so reluctant to live with someone earlier. One day, the truth struck me all of a sudden: I had not trusted that I could live through childbirth. My mother had almost died in bearing my little brother. I feared that very much. It was only, therefore, after my child-bearing years that I let myself get intimate, truly intimate, with a man.   [July 1984]

Seven of the 30 women reported that their comparison of men who had asked them to marry with men or women friends whom they saw in a regular way cast a shadow on the marital prospect. The 7 experienced friendship as ensuring intimacy without subordination; they gauged marriage to be a condition of subordination without a guarantee of intimacy. One woman articulated this point of view in the following way:

So I had the chance to marry a bunch of times. But why would I marry when I had everything I wanted without that? I saw my friends every day. I always had people to share my good times and hardships with. Why would I marry someone who may or may not turn out to be a friend? I would be connected for life to someone who might not be as fine a companion as Sarah and Harry, my buddies since elementary school. And I knew that it is difficult to keep up friendships in a first-rate and timely way once you owe best energy to a husband. [May 1982]

Preference for familial intimacy over that which marriage might offer helped shape the decision to remain single for 8 of the 30 women. They were women who described their childhood as a particularly happy time and their ongoing adult bonds with their parents or siblings as the most meaningful of their lives. A woman reflected:

> Many said I was "married to my family." They were not wrong. My brothers, Joe and Frank, were the dearest people you would ever want to meet. They were joyous to be with. We shared everything. None of us three ever got married because outsiders looked pale by comparison with the other two of us. Oh, I know, I've read what head doctors would say about us. "We had unresolved, incestuous feelings for each other." But that is simply wrong. We did not want each other physically; we wanted only to share everything else: spirit, mind, emotions, and daily life. And we did that. When the flesh got weak, each of us had friends who would come calling. I suppose we were "free lovers" but we didn't think of ourselves in that way. We just felt that you didn't have to marry to enjoy the best of companionship. [August 1983]

Those 4 women whose commitment to parents was their strongest bond sounded equally impassioned. Though born into a Freudian age, such women, like the one who made the following comments, were quite open about their preference for keeping close to parents rather than marrying:

> Do you know how many amateur psychiatrists have told me that my attachment to Mother and Father was "unnatural"? If keeping a good thing when you have it is "unnatural," so be it. I loved them so. They provided more fun and excitement than any four men I dated.

They never got in my way when I wished to entertain some gentleman. They also neither encouraged nor discouraged me from marrying.

Mother would now and then say: "Just don't shame us, darling." That meant, be discreet and don't get pregnant. I was and didn't! [July 1982]

Some women explained their choice to remain single by suggesting that they wanted to remain childless. Two women believed that they would not have made good parents; 5 women reported that raising children did not interest them, though they found other people's children enjoyable "in limited doses." Clearly, these 7 women did not trust that they could marry and refrain from having children. In response to my questions about this assumption that marriage entailed childraising, one woman responded:

Maybe since *The Second Sex* and *The Feminine Mystique* have been read by many people, women feel freer to talk and think about their ambivalence about having children. But, child, please remember that I became thirty in 1929. Who, then, aside from French intellectuals and Greenwich Village radicals, expressed such revolutionary thoughts? Why, wasn't the very pillar of our culture motherhood and devotion to children? To reject such a thing was like spitting at God.

So, to think of marrying in 1929 without assuming that children would follow was most unorthodox. Both men who wanted to marry me wanted children very much. Most people did then. By not marrying, I did not have to put up with the hints, jokes, winks, and lectures that my married friends endured when they hadn't "produced" by the third year of their marriage. No one urges a single women to have babies, especially a middle-class black woman like myself. My people wanted me to teach and uplift my race. White people wanted me to help stanch the torrent of black babies, not add to it! [September 1983]

For reasons of ideological commitment, 4 of the 50 women did not marry. Of these women, 2 explained their opposition to marriage in self-consciously feminist terms. They understood the role of wife to be inherently oppressive. One woman explained it this way:

I was not born, nor was anyone born, to be a wife. A wife is chattel. She is supposed to place herself second to her man, to serve him. All this mumbo jumbo about "liberated marriages" is bunk. Men gain from marriage; women lose. They give away their birthright of freedom for the sake of security and social status, only to find out that the promises are false. [January 1983]

Another woman opposed marriage on anarchistic grounds:

I have spent seventy-three years fighting authoritarianism. Emma Goldman's writings inspired me at a young age to consider carefully and critically the implications of marriage. It seemed to me, after much study, thought, and observation of married women around me, that to marry is to uphold a social form that helps few and oppresses many. I don't even think it serves men. They become ciphers, too, of an institution that reduces people to hackneyed roles and postures. [November 1982]

Another woman, who also refused to marry for political reasons, struck a socialist chord:

> You wonder why I did not marry? Why not ask me something hard? That one's easy to answer. Marriage makes women into property. Why should workers of the world unite only to be oppressed or oppressive in their personal relationships? Marriage makes tools of men and women. It makes them instruments alienated from each other. I love men. I wish to be close to them. What quicker way to put distance between yourself and a male friend than to marry him and to thereby introduce propertarian obstacles into a relationship? [March 1984]

Devotion encouraged 2 women to join religious orders that required celibacy. One woman became a member of a Catholic order; the other joined a Methodist missionary effort in China. Both made a conscious choice to leave secular life, although each considered marriage offers before going into the religious life. Their spiritual commitment appears to have been the pivotal force that moved them into their respective orders. The Methodist missionary discussed her singleness this way:

> People often write or say that members of religious orders are yielding to family pressure, avoiding men (or women), hiding from sex, or escaping the responsibilities of making a living. Well, none of those explanations apply to me. The only thing that compelled me to become a missionary was that it was God's will. My family was opposed to it. They wondered why I couldn't serve God as a Christian wife and mother. Once I be-

came one, the only thing that kept me a missionary in the most difficult of conditions was God's will. Life would have been far easier as a wife and mother. Those who think of missionary work as escape ought to try it for eight months. They'll know better after the first epidemic of typhoid. [June 1984]

Predictably, the 12 women I interviewed who were single involuntarily provide a less rosy picture of never-married life than do the 38 women who chose their unmarried status. Of these 12 women, 7 reported that conflicts between care-giving responsibilities for elderly parents and the demands of fiances ended their marriage plans. All 7 expressed some degree of bitterness over the loss of their marital prospects—but none of them, interestingly enough, regretted acting as a caretaker. They resented, instead, their perceived abandonment by other siblings when care for a parent or parents was needed. They also resented the inflexibility of their suitors. One woman's comment is representative:

I alone took care of Papa. He was sick for three and one-half years during his last bout with cancer. I was seeing Joe at that time. Joe helped me a great deal with my father. For a long time, he understood when I couldn't leave Papa alone, when I couldn't go out in the evening or on a weekend. After two years of that, Joe asked me to make some changes. He wanted me to get my brother to take care of Papa more often. You see, he knew we didn't have any money to pay for a companion. And, back then, there wasn't any social security or Medicare to pay for help with.

My brother couldn't or wouldn't help. Joe got more and more frustrated. Finally, he told me that I had to put my father in a home if he was going to marry me. The only homes we could afford were disgusting. I refused, and, after awhile, Joe stopped coming by. [August 1983]

This woman, like the other 6 who reported similar tensions between responsibilities to aging parents and socializing with potential mates, came to terms with her singleness by the age of forty. All 7 reported that they knew they were past "marriageable age" by then. (Three of the 7 thought that age thirty-five was the upper limit for marrying.) These women have spent the second half of their lives shaping a single existence after thinking, throughout the first half, that they would marry. Each of the seven found the transition years, between the ages thirty and forty, to be the most trying period of their lives. During those years, they performed difficult care-taking while holding full-time paid jobs, sacrificed relationships they deemed desirable, and learned to view themselves as unmarried women in a culture that considered that status tantamount to failure. Small wonder that these 7 women internalized this social judgment and considered themselves, to greater or lesser degree, *manqué*. Some did so with considerable humor. As one woman commented ironically: "I am clearly one of America's unclaimed treasures."

The only pitiable woman of the 50 I interviewed was the one who had wished to marry when she was much younger and who believed that she was single because she was "too ugly to catch a man." The only one who bore serious emotional scars, she exhibited a form of self-contempt that stemmed from a highly troubled childhood, compounded by her single status, which, to her, was proof of her inherent undesirability.

Far more self-accepting and philosophical about single life were the 4 women with disabilities who, earlier in their lives, would have liked to have married. Disabled by polio, without the use of her legs since she was twelve, one woman had worked full-time, sustained a rich social life, and lived with a long-term lover whom she refused to marry because she felt she was not physically capable of being a competent mother. Similar courage and flexibility were evident in the life of a woman with severe disability from cerebral palsy, who came to realize that her physical limitations and disfigurement made marriage improbable. This woman, a particularly self-reflective person, reported that she had consciously compensated for the lack of a desired husband and children by "investing" deeply in friends and in her very successful career as an academician and researcher. Two other women, one with severe hemophilia and the other with epilepsy, had decided in their late twenties that it was best not to marry, so as to avoid bearing children with the same physical conditions. The woman who had epilepsy commented:

> In those years, to have epilepsy was to have a real curse. People looked at you funny when they knew. I couldn't get a job, despite my college degree, because employers just didn't hire epileptics then for fear you would have an attack at the wrong time, or because they thought you were mentally sick, or maybe because they were afraid of medical claims if an attack happened at work. I finally got a job, at age twenty-seven, in the office of a shoe factory through a college friend. And a good thing it was for me, too, because I knew that I would have to support myself all my life since I *would not* marry and reproduce these trials in my sons or daughters. [July 1983]

Aside from single status, perhaps the most common thread of identity shared by many of the women was their view of themselves as members of a group *larger than* their own families. When asked what had brought meaning to their lives, 45 of the women emphasized contributions they had made or were still making to a "serving" profession, a volunteer group, religious congregation, or political organization or cause. One expression of this commitment follows:

> All Puerto Rican kids are *my* family. If I had to name one thing in life I am proud of, it is my twenty-three years of volunteering for the Puerto Rican version of "Big Sisters." Of those sixteen children I have been a buddy to over the years, not one of them has gotten into trouble. If that organization had not been around, I would have had to create it. Just for my own good. [September 1983]

At first glance, this desire to contribute to society appears to be much like the desire to serve that Martha Vicinus found among British single women, born in the mid-nineteenth century, who became teachers, professors, nurses, social reformers, and suffragists. Like their nineteenth-century counterparts, these contemporary single women conceive of themselves as part of a community of contributors, members of a "family" that incorporates "brothers and sisters" who are in some way vulnerable, or share a similar spiritual vision or the same racial background, or profess common political ideals. Yet, unlike their single predecessors of a century past, these twentieth-century women do *not* view their service to others as emblematic of a vocation peculiar to single women. Instead, they see this committed activity as a moral or political vocation that flows from their membership in humanity, rather than from their gender and marital status. Like the earlier single women, they seek to expand their experience and influence beyond the confines of their family of origin through service. Unlike the nineteenth-century women, their "mission" springs from their sense of commonality with diverse others.

Vicinus has written of nineteenth-century single women's devotion to service:

> The spinster had thrust upon her absolute purity and goodness. She was supposed to remain virginal and utterly self-sacrificing for all who needed her. Single women transformed their passive role into one of active spirituality and passionate social service. Celibacy, within the context of loving friendships, became a vital and empowering ideal.[11]

For the 45 twentieth-century single women I interviewed who emphasized their involvement in society, neither virginity nor self-sacrifice was linked to their social service, except in the cases of the two women who are members of religious communities. Whereas the nineteenth-century women constructed their lives in an era that proclaimed the doctrine of essentialism—in this case, belief in inherent moral differences between the genders and in the moral superiority of women—the twentieth-century women have gone "beyond separate spheres" to an integrationist and social-constructionist perspective.[12] They see themselves as equal to and, morally speaking, identical with men in their responsibility for constructing themselves and their environment. As moral human beings, they understand themselves, like men and married women, to be responsible for the welfare and continuing survival of the human species.

This sense of responsibility is manifest in the daily lives of the women who were interviewed. The 45 women who take part in religious, political, or humanitarian activities contribute on an average of 18.3 hours each week to the cause or causes of their choice. For most of the 45, their contributions are now strictly voluntary. Earlier in their lives, the women who were service professionals—as teacher, social worker, nurse, librarian, or doctor—intertwined their social or spiritual concerns with their paid work.

A very active group of people, these never-married women have approached paid work, community commitments, and volunteering with the greatest seriousness. They have acted throughout their lives as people with twentieth-century versions of a "calling," a term Robert Bellah has recently reframed in *Habits of the Heart*.[13] These single women think of themselves as members of an integrated moral world in which their commitments to their work, their family, their friends, their neighborhood, and their society flow from one passion—the desire to be a responsible and responsive actor in the world.

Just as their "calling" directly influenced the lifestyle preferences of those who chose single life, so did their pragmatic recognition of the constraints placed upon them by a patriarchal culture. Most of the women I interviewed, like the professional single women of Accra, Ghana, studied by Carmel Dinan, did not directly challenge male privilege in the family or workplace. Instead, these American women sought to minimize their oppression by avoiding marriage. In Dinan's words, as pragmatists rather than feminists, professional single women in Ghana "acknowledge male superordination and concentrate energies on finding self-fulfilling solutions within existing structures."[14]

Nine of the 50 never-married women *did* refer to themselves as feminists. They spoke with fervor about inequities that women encounter at work, in the family, and at the hands of the state. All 9, of whom 4 had stated explicitly that opposition to marriage as an institution had led them to remain single, had performed political work on a feminist issue of importance to them. Three of them had worked for the cause of reproductive rights. (One of these 3, a teacher, had helped some teenage students obtain abortions by paying a physician to perform the operations in her apartment in the late 1930s and early 1940s, when abortions were illegal, dangerous, and costly.) Two others had fought wage discrimination against women at their workplace; 2 had worked as members of the National Organization for Women, in support of the Equal Rights Amendment; one had singlehandedly (and successfully) challenged the exclusion of girls from the prime hours of a local, public playground's tennis courts; and one had raised money for a neighborhood shelter for abused wives.

Only these 4 women, who explicitly opposed marriage as a "keystone of male supremacy," as one put it, understood her own choice of single status to be a feminist act. Most of the 50 women interpreted singlehood as the best possible individual manipulation of a marriage system that appeared less than desirable to her.

Perhaps the many women who had chosen singleness for other than political reasons and did not define themselves as feminists can best be viewed as both pragmatists and protofeminists. They are pragmatists in their individualistic approach to sidestepping subordination through remaining single, without consciously desiring to or working to overthrow the hegemony of marriage. They are, at the same time, protofeminists in their discontent with male privilege within the marital relation and in their efforts to create a way of life in which, as single women of independent dignity, they can serve as "models to be reached by the average women we everyday meet," just as Susan B. Anthony declared a century ago.

Another essential component of the 50 women's definitions of "self" was their identification as members of their particular generations, those born between 1884 and 1918. This identification has two parts, according to gerontologist Matilda White Riley: a life-course dimension and a historical dimension.[15] The first part concerns the woman's place, at the time of the interview, in the age structure of society and in the flow of her overall life. The women who were interviewed saw themselves as retired people, as members of the oldest third of American society, and as individuals completing the final third of their lives. Many, however, did not view themselves as "old." Only 12 of the 50 women thought of themselves as "old"; 38 rejected the label "old" and, instead, understood themselves to be simply "older" than other people. One woman of ninety-five commented:

> I'm a long way from old. I'll be old when I no longer feel lively. And I'm very lively, despite my bad eyes and knees. Some young people are old. Some old people are young. The label can't be applied from the outside. It has to be attached from within by the only one living inside my skin and my soul—me.   [June 1984]

The second part of generational identity involves a person's sense of location in the course of history. Karl Mannheim conceptualized this as "generational consciousness," a modification of Dilthey's notion of "contemporaneity," the inner unity of a generation that is the subjective condition of having been submitted to the same determining influences.[16] The women I interviewed seemed acutely aware of the respective generations into which they were born. In reflecting on their lives, they relied much more on historical markers than on their own birthdays to help them recall the sequence of their activities and relationships. When I would ask: "At what age did you first consider yourself a woman who might not marry?" the response was often similar to one woman's answer: "Let's see, the war ended in 1918, so I must have been twenty-one when I first thought about staying single permanently."

In interpreting their lives, the women tended to highlight historical events and influences, such as the two World Wars and the
Great Depression, more than life-course changes. They seldom re-
ferred to life stages (such as middle age or old age) or to transitions
between life stages. They made many references to the impact of
historical forces on their lives. Several, however, noted the importance of the intersection of a particular life stage with a historical
moment. For example, one woman thought it highly significant to
her career's configuration that she began teaching in 1931, economically grim as that era was. Another woman noted that she had
come to adulthood in 1917, just as the United States entered
World War I, affording her opportunities to train and travel that
she would otherwise not have had. Many commented on the
importance of having spent their childhood in an age when their
parents' and grandparents' views on sex, gender roles, and childraising were still Victorian. Several black women noted the short
time between their first year of life and the slavery of their parents or grandparents.

In identifying with a particular generation, the 50 women re-
ferred to a combination of objective and subjective influences that
they deemed significant to their life chances and choices. They considered the climates of opinion when they were children and young
adults to be crucial. They identified shifts in labor-market supply
and demand as important in helping to shape their generations'
possibilities. They thought the wages and technology available to
women born in their times were important determinants. Occupational segregation by gender and race in America's work force left
them, they felt, few job or career choices.

Many women noted the significance of the decline in the number of fatal diseases during their life time and vividly remembered
the deaths of relatives and friends in an earlier era from sicknesses
that no longer kill. Their generation's encounters, as teenagers or

young adults, with international events—wars and the Depression, in particular—seemed critical to these women. So did certain social movements. Many women considered the rise of the Congress of Industrial Organizations, the civil rights movement, and the women's movement important factors that influenced their opportunities and conditions.

Without question, the movement most frequently cited as transforming their generations' daily lives, particularly in comparison with the lives of their parents' generations, was the New Deal legislation. Social security, Aid to Families with Dependent Children (welfare), workers' compensation, and unemployment insurance provided a shield—no matter how inadequate—between the self-sufficiency of the employed single woman and her potential impoverishment due to old age, sickness, injury on the job, or unemployment.

All but 2 of the women I spoke with had supported their parents, totally or partially, during their old age. The 2 exceptions were economically privileged women whose parents had been able to save and invest for their own retirement years. During the Great Depression, 17 of the 50 women were the chief breadwinners for their parents, as well as themselves, for two years or longer, due to their fathers' loss of work and inability to find another job. Forty-eight women were acutely aware that their childlessness would have left them dependent on friends, relatives, or the state during illness in middle or old age, if not for the social legislation of the 1930s. Perhaps it was no coincidence that 7 women (14 percent of the sample) permanently displayed photographs or portraits of Franklin Delano Roosevelt in their living rooms.

Medicare and Medicaid programs, begun in 1965, were almost equal in importance to the New Deal in creating a profoundly different aging experience for the generations represented by these women than for those of their parents. Such provisions enabled all but the 6 oldest women to buy health care services and medications from the time of their retirement, at sixty-three, sixty-five, or older. Most of the women had difficult memories of an era in which medical funds for their parents' old age came from the pockets of relatives, or not at all. One woman remembered:

> When Dad got sick, I took a second job. Mom went to work at age sixty, though she had never had a paid job before in her life. Still that wasn't enough to cover the operations. So I cleared out my savings that I was keeping for old age. Still that wasn't near enough. We begged the rest of the family for help, much as we hated to go hat in hand in that manner. We sold furniture. Mom sold her wedding ring and jewelry that Dad had given her over the years. When Dad died, Mom and I were $11,000 in debt to the hospital and doctors. It took me nine years to dig my way out of that. [January 1983]

Alert to attitudinal, economic, and political forces that have played on people of their generations, these single women presented illuminating analyses of the intersection of history and biography in their own lives. They showed particular sensitivity to the contrasts in economic security and technological sophistication between their parents' generation and their own. However, though the women felt, for the most part, luckier than their parents in terms of social insurance and technology, they did not view history as a stream of unending, linear progress. Nor did they appear to romanticize the Victorian and Edwardian periods of their parents. Their conversation was rich with comments on the tradeoffs that twentieth-century actors must make in order to enjoy the fruits of the New Deal and of the television and airplane era.

With few exceptions, these women view themselves as robust individuals who, having purposefully sidestepped marriage, have had to grapple throughout adulthood with the challenge of balancing autonomy and intimacy outside the prescribed marital roles. For many, this balancing act has required a high degree of self-awareness that proves, as we shall see, advantageous in old age.

THREE / Family

I'm surprised you haven't asked me if my family was highly protective. Most people assume that a single woman has been sheltered near to suffocation. In fact, my parents urged me to take every risk in the book. Why, when I was five, my father and mother sent me to spend summers with an uncle who ran a tourist hotel in the Adirondacks. They wanted me to learn early that I could get along fine on my own. When other girls' parents were forbidding them to see boys yet, my parents were encouraging it. They used to say: "Life is short, Tina. Explore every inch of it."   [January 1984]

A commonly held prejudgment of single old women is that their families kept them from living fully or that the women themselves hid behind their families to escape men, sex, work, children, or the unexpected. The 50 autobiographical stories presented to me suggest that the problem of overprotection was encountered by only a few of the group of 50. For most of these never-married women, as for most people, families were a mixed blessing. The women reported finding protection *and* challenge in their families of origin, encouraging *and* undermining signals, constraints *and* opportunities. Predictably, most women recalled more readily the support they received from kin than the troubles they experienced with them.

> My father's face has been before me since I was a little child. He's dead now, thirty-two years, but he's still my main source of inspiration. We had such a good time together, my father and mother and us four kids. But it was much more than a good time. Our family was a bedrock of security, yet it was also a demanding place. The family demanded that everybody become as much as they could and contribute as much as possible. The standards were high, but so were the rewards I got for being with those grand people.   [March 1983]

For this woman, her family had been a fountainhead of meaning, encouragement, and closeness. She spoke with obvious feeling about the richness of her childhood of seventy-five years ago. In analyzing the kinds of support she derived from her family of origin, she, like many of the women interviewed, acknowledged the example a parent—in this case her father—had provided of conscientious and joyful living.

Thirty-eight of the women volunteered such a story of their family of origin: 14 saw their fathers as central; 21 their mothers; and 3 both their parents. Twelve women in the study did *not* view their parent or parents as sources of primary identity. Of those, 9 identified other adults as the most salient role models; 3 said they had no such figures in their conscious past.

One woman articulated, in detail, the dimensions of the mimetic process she experienced as both a child and a young adult in relation to her mother:

> Do you know what it is like to have a noble mother, one who genuinely cares about the world around her as well as about the welfare of her family and herself? My mother was *not* larger than life. She had a quick temper. She was messy. She had trouble admitting when she was wrong. She often got into fights that were unnecessary. But she was noble.
>
> She taught me that one must make a contribution in one's very own way. She taught me that life without fun in it is thin and mean. She showed me about the gives and takes of relationships. She taught me about courage in the way that she decided to study to become a lawyer when she was fifty-four, despite my father's opposition and despite the nine law schools that turned her down cold. She just kept applying and reapplying, until one school took her in. Mind you, this is a woman whose only other work had been as a clerk-typist for twelve years, before she had me. How could I miss having a good life with that kind of example to follow? [June 1982]

Parents also helped sustain the identities of many of these 50 women when they were past childhood and well on their way to adulthood, middle age, or old age. In sharp contrast to the single men studied by sociologists Alan Davis and Philip Strong, most of the never-married women whom I interviewed did *not* lack "interactional confirmatory devices," people with whom "to rehearse their identity."[1] Almost half the women reported *daily* contact or extended phone calls with either a parent or sibling until the death of that relative. Another 9 women indicated that they initiated or received visits from a parent or sibling *at least twice a week*. One woman recollects:

> Until just two years ago, I saw my sister Gladys every single day since we were children, except, of course, when one of us was away on vacation. She lived a few blocks away from here. We were very different people, Gladys and I, but that only helped us to stay close. After all, who wants to look in the mirror all of the time?
>
> Gladys was married and had three boys. So she particularly looked forward to that hour or two with me each day in which she did not have to be wife or mother. You see, with me she was just Gladys. Now I got lots out of this arrangement. I got a close, close companion with whom I shared my innermost thoughts, fears, and hopes. Nobody ever had a better friend than Gladys was to me. I say "was," because she dropped dead two years ago of a heart attack. She cannot be replaced.   [November 1983]

A surprising number reported that their families placed extraordinary faith in them.

Mother thought I could accomplish anything I set my mind to. She told me that about four times a day from the time I was an infant. When I wanted to learn German, she fought with the school system until they put me in a school that taught that language. When I wanted to learn to play baseball, she and Father found an older boy on our block to teach me, since neither of them had played baseball in Italy when they were children. She believed in me completely. Consequently, it never occurred to me to do otherwise myself. [March 1984]

Others recalled that their families gave them unusual support for independent behavior. One woman described her adolescence in these terms:

All my friends used to come talk to my father when we were in high school. He was such a wise man. When people told me that I might not catch a man if I remained so independent, he would laugh and say: "Bertha, if you want a man, you'll find one that loves you *and* your independence. Don't change a thing." In fact, when senior prom time came, he encouraged me to ask a boy I had a special feeling for. I told him that no girls did that. He told me that it was about time they started. He was like that all the fifty-six years I knew him, but that free-thinking spirit of his was never more of a help to me than in those years between sixteen and twenty-one, when everybody around me was trying to "should" me to death, or at least into courtship. [February 1983]

Encouragement to follow their own paths came from family members during adulthood as well. Nineteen of the 50 women initiated comments on the support they received from relatives in the years between ages thirty and forty. For these 19, that decade of life presented particularly serious strains because it was the first time in which they remembered being looked at as anomalies, as women who had moved beyond the threshold of marriageability. In their twenties, they reported that they were still viewed as women "holding out." In their thirties, they were viewed, as one woman put it, as "leftovers." She also noted:

> Do you know how fine it is to have a mother who doesn't care about what the neighbors think? She thought I led a thoroughly splendid life. She took such pride in my nursing and "adventures." Once when I came to visit her when I was approximately thirty-five, her brother, my Uncle Harry, made some crack about how I was withering on the vine. Before I could answer, my mother was all over him. She sat him down and bragged about me for two hours. She ended the lecture by saying, "Harry, if that's what withering on the vine is like, let's have lots more of it in this family. She's the happiest one of us all." [May 1984]

Middle age was another period in which these women remembered being buoyed by the encouragement of family members. One woman, who lost her hearing in her mid-forties, remembers:

> My two brothers were godsends when my hearing went. I could not have kept my job and daily routines without them. They arranged all sorts of things for me when I

was too low to do it for myself. They got somebody to teach me how to lipread. They encouraged my boss to learn sign language along with me. (He did, by the way. He couldn't bear to lose me, he said.) They scoured the literature for new gadgets available for the deaf. I hope I have been as good a sister to them as they have been loyal brothers to me.   [August 1984]

A different sort of support emerged in middle age for another woman:

When I was fifty-two, Grace died. She and I had lived together since we were college roommates. I was desperate with grief for more than a year. In the first period of my mourning, my sister came by every day. She and I never discussed the nature of my relationship with Grace, because she was afraid it was unseemly. But she knew that Grace had meant everything to me and so comforted me accordingly. It is a rare person who can pull off such an act of generosity in the face of her own fears and doubts.   [July 1982]

Old age was also a time of life in which many of the women obtained crucial support from their families. The support was in some cases emotional, in others financial, in still others physical. A woman with severe arthritis said:

When my arthritis gets bad I call my sister for help. She helps me clean and cook and shop. We've a good arrangement because I have more money than she does, so I pay her for her work with me. Also, having been a bookkeeper for forty-one years, I am able to keep her accounts for her, to pay her bills, and assist her with her tax return. Each hand washes the other, leaving both of us better off and nobody indebted. [March 1984]

One important way in which family members lent aid to the women I interviewed was through sharing a household after retirement. Of the 50 women interviewed, 23 *began* living in an apartment or house with a sister or brother during retirement. Another 8 women continued to live with a sibling after retiring. These 31 women who shared a household with a brother or sister in old age did so for a wide range of reasons. They were economizing because of their fixed incomes, helping each other with the tasks of everyday life, and providing mutual assistance in times of sickness. They were also ensuring companionship at a time of life when friends, neighbors, lovers, and relatives become fewer in number because of institutionalization and death, and when social interaction in general declines because the process of retirement obliterates a major source of acquaintances and face-to-face exchange. One of the 31 women who lived with a sister or brother in her old age reported:

As mandatory retirement got closer and closer, my dollars saved looked fewer and fewer. Jim, my favorite brother, suggested that we take an apartment together. He reasoned that two pensions would stretch farther than one. He was by that point a widower of seven years. I weighed in my mind the pros and cons and decided that I would sacrifice some of my independence in order to gain a companion for my old age. My two closest friends were a decade or so older than me and were already thinking about retirement communities. I was not interested in that at seventy. Jim's offer looked more appealing, at least until such time that I was no longer fully functioning. [January 1983]

Companionship was offered by family members to many of the women long before old age. Thirty-two of the women had very frequent contact with relatives. Of these, 21 women had lived with a parent or sibling for ten years or more of their life before age sixty-five. Nonetheless, most women identified old age as the life stage in which they most relied upon family members for company. One woman expressed her reliance on family ties in this way:

I lost my three most intimate buddies in the space of five years. Those three were the people whom I had shared everything with since I was first employed at Smith's in 1931. It was a stunning loss that is impossible to describe in words. I reeled from those deaths for a while and spent a lot of time alone and lonesome.

Then I took stock of my situation and decided to make the best of things. The next-best thing to those friends were my sisters. I asked them both to consider renting a three-bedroom apartment with me. They were each widows who were delighted with the prospect. We lived together as a trio for twelve years, until Maddy had to go to a nursing home when her mind caved in. Susan and I continued living together until last year, when she died of stomach cancer. The three of us did pretty well. We had our spats, but basically got along in jolly fashion. [September 1982]

For the 12 black women I interviewed, their families of origin had indeed served as "havens in a heartless world."[2] Without exception, all 12 women reported that their families had supported them in many ways throughout their lives, despite the puzzlement, even disappointment, that the parents of 7 of these women had expressed to them about their never-married state. Each of the 12 black women reported having been included in and aided by extended kin systems of aunts, uncles, grandparents, and cousins, in addition to their immediate families. The help they received was material, emotional, and spiritual. One woman articulated very clearly the diversity of support she received from her extended family:

> I lived near my own people all my life. Some of them didn't understand why I didn't have a man. Now and then they would poke at me about that. But I didn't pay that any mind since I knew what a firm place I had in their hearts. I gave a lot to them, but I got even more back.
>
> When I was sick, they took care of me. If I ran short of food, somebody brought some over. When I needed a dress to go look for work in, one of my aunts or sisters came up with one. When money was short, they provided. If I was low, they cheered me up. When I got arrested for using a white washroom, they bailed me out and made a hero of me for it.   [June 1984]

The 12 black women came from different social classes. Three had parents who were tenant farmers; 4 were raised by parents who were domestic workers, handymen, and laundresses; 2 had parents who were small shopkeepers; and 3 were daughters of ministers or teachers. The similarity of familial experience reported by these women of differing class origins lends support to sociologist Harriette Pipes McAdoo's finding that the kin-help networks of extended black families in the United States permeate not only poor black families, but black working- and middle-class families as well.[3]

The 4 Puerto Rican Americans interviewed described deep involvement and reliance on their families of origin throughout their adulthood. They had been raised in low-income, extended families in which intergenerational interdependency was encouraged and independent household arrangements were discouraged.[4] Three of the women lived with their extended families; one lived several blocks from her parents' apartment. This report seems to reflect the experiences of all 4 women:

> Living in my family is like living in an anthill. Everyone has an assignment to help the family out with, so we scurry around doing so. There is constant motion and talk. Why, the last time I remember a moment of silence in my family was when John Kennedy was killed, and we were all too shocked to speak.
>
> Nothing goes unnoticed or unassisted in my family. When I lost my job at Dolfinger's in 1965, they supported me until I could find another one. When I was thinking about retiring, my brother and sister bought me a cruise to celebrate. When I look sick, somebody in the family insists that I go to the doctor. When I was caring for Mama in her last days, people cooked for me and cleaned for me. When I get short, somebody helps me pay the bills. Now, of course, every penny I earned and all my social security goes directly to the family kitty. So I feel good about taking from that same kitty. My family, you must understand, has taken an interest in everything I do, and I, in return, involve myself with their every concern. [March 1983]

The one woman from a Cuban family came from an upper-middle-class background. Her father had been a physician and her mother a psychologist. Her family was deeply involved with her welfare and everyday affairs. However, this interest in her daily life appears to have been counterbalanced by a sensitivity to her desire to have some privacy. For example, she reported that family members always phoned to ask permission to visit. She remembered immersion in an extended kin network in Havana, but said that network fragmented when the family migrated to Philadelphia in 1958. This woman described her family during the years in the United States as being much more nuclear in form and dynamics than before:

> Even here, I found I could lean on my family for almost everything. But in the United States that means leaning on five relatives rather than on twenty or twenty-five people, as I would have back home. Five isn't many, but this five is an able and loving lot. It's not so easy to set up a new life, as I did, at age fifty-three when we moved here. But my parents and sisters and I held together like glue. Those of us still alive are as close as ever.   [February 1984]

Like the woman from Cuba, the two Asian-American women were embedded in extended kin systems for the first portion of their lives. In the face of voluntary or forced migration, these arrangements collapsed, and they were left with a much smaller family circle from which they drew economic and social support. One of these women, born in China in 1901 into a peasant family, reported that her entire small village, in which she lived until 1939, was in some way related to her. Upon moving to an American city, she recalled that her surrounding family "was no longer numerous like the stars in the heavens on a clear night. My family dwindled to the size of a tiny constellation."

Similarly, the Japanese-American woman recalled the breakup of her extended family. Born into a southern California extended family of Issei (those who had migrated from Japan) farmers, she, together with twenty-seven other family members, was herded into a Nisei relocation camp immediately after Pearl Harbor. In 1946, her family was dispersed again by government officials, to New Jersey, to Oregon, and to Iowa. At age thirty-six, this woman went to live in south Jersey with her parents and one sister, where the four of them worked in a seafood processing plant. She remembers her family's support in the fifteen years she lived in New Jersey:

> We had only each other then. They had taken our land and our livelihood from us. They had put us in the camp for five years. That was terrible. But the worst part was having the family split up by the government officials who sent us all over the country. With all that to endure, we made a solemn family vow when we got to Oceanflow in New Jersey that nobody and no government would break the four of us up. We stayed together through mother's, then father's death.
>
> My sister and I went everywhere together until she got sick three years ago. Before that, we were inseparable. We worked at the same place, lived in the same house, and retired at the same time. Family means an inestimable amount to someone like me who has seen one's relatives sent away to places too far to visit in parts of the countryside where there is no Japanese-American community or culture whatsoever. [May 1983]

By contrast, the Native American woman whom I interviewed chose to distance herself from both her immediate family and her extended kin network, though she had found them strongly supportive of her teenage desire to go to college and prepare for social work. Their assumption had been that she would return to the Navaho reservation in New Mexico on which she had been raised and apply her training to the health and welfare needs of her people. She had entered college and a school of social work with that goal in mind. Yet, as she lived, trained, and worked in urban, East Coast areas, she grew fond of the autonomy and mobility of big-city life. She remained in the East, but not without some inner conflict over her isolation from her family and, in particular, from her elders. Throughout much of her adulthood, this woman identified distance from the older members of her kin system as a condition of anomie and culturelessness.[5] She expressed her longing for familial support and proximity this way:

> I have led a fine and full life here in the East. Otherwise I would have gone back. Yet a void yawns whenever I think of my grandparents and parents. They gave me total love when I was a child. Now they have all died without my knowing them well since I have grown up. That is akin to not knowing oneself and one's history.
>
> I am old now myself, eighty-two. But to be old is not to be an elder. Elders are people who keep the Navaho tradition alive through teaching our values to the next generations. I have not done that. I have taught values, but not Navaho ideals. That can only be done in the lap of one's family.   [February 1983]

In investigating family networks, it is as important to avoid idealizing kin relations as it is to avoid underestimating them. The familial demands on these 50 women were broad and deep. Both the costs and benefits of these demands merit attention. In some cases, families exacted heavy tolls, as the following woman's comments reveal:

> Mother developed bad arthritis and could no longer take charge of her household. So, of course, as the only one of her children still living at home, I took responsibility for running the house and taking care of my mother. Father was around, but he was of no real use when it came to cooking, cleaning, or assisting Mother.
>
> Mother gave up managing the house when I was forty-one. She died four years ago, soon after my seventieth birthday. A bit of simple arithmetic will tell you that I cared for her for twenty-nine years. Father, in the midst of all that, got sick as well, for three years. He needed me as much as Mother did for awhile, until the cancer took him. I felt like Florence Nightingale in the Crimea, except that I never got famous for nursing, like she did. I just got tired. Don't forget, I was working during all those years full-time until I reached seventy. [January 1982]

Managing the family household and caring for elderly parents were common responsibilities shouldered by these never-married women. Not "designated daughters," a term coined by Patricia Palmieri to describe middle-class, single women born in the mid- and late-nineteenth century who were "exempted from the norms of domesticity and were designated for achievement," these informants were called upon for many family duties.[6] Thirty-six of the 50 women took charge of their family homes or apartments for periods of at least five years. Of these 36, 16 lived at home without interruption from childhood; 20 reentered the family household when a parent was physically dependent upon them. These 20 women did so either alone or (in 9 cases) accompanied by a friend who also moved into the family residence.

An even higher proportion of these single women served as care-givers for their aged parents. Forty-two of the 50 women were the primary caretaker of an ailing parent. As a number of studies have demonstrated, providing care to elderly, dependent family members is "women's work."[7] The reflections of these 42 women would suggest that care-giving is never-married women's work when a single daughter is available in the family. One woman recounted:

> We never talked about who would take care of Dad when he got sick. All of us assumed, me included, that I would do it. My two brothers were busy with their work and families. My older sister had three children to take care of. So I was the natural choice, having nothing but my job to look after. [August 1984]

In the words of British sociologists Davis and Strong, single people are viewed by their families as "free-floating resources," as the family members most vulnerable to the plight of their parents because they "can't counterbalance [family claims] with claims of their own partners and children. Women in particular are at risk here. . . . Women are more expected to display such filial sacrifice."[8] Not only were the women I interviewed expected to display such filial sacrifice, they expected it of themselves, in 40 of the 42 instances. As one of the 40 said:

> I couldn't have lived with myself if I hadn't done my bit to care for Mom. My two sisters had their hands full

with children and husbands. I was always the one Mom had turned to anyways, since Dad died. If she could care for me in my first sixteen years, it only seems fair that I should care for her in her last days. [November 1983]

Only 2 of the 42 never-married care-givers felt coerced into care-giving. They resented the responsibility, their siblings' lack of assistance in providing care, and their family's presupposition of their availability, as a single woman, to be on call for family demands. Each stated that she would have been willing to share the work of caring for an elderly parent with other family members.

I had a very demanding job. I had a rich network of friends that I saw regularly. But when Papa got sick, everybody but me took it for granted that I should take care of him. Nobody seemed to notice the significance nor complexity of the life I had created for myself. It was as if my existence was invisible because it didn't take place under a marriage canopy.

Papa needed constant attention, more than any one person could possibly devote without giving up everything else. Had my brothers and sisters done their part, I could have contributed to the work and expense of taking care of my father without sacrificing my job and my social life. But whenever I turned to my sisters, they would say something that translated into: "I'm too busy being a wife and mother to help." Whenever I turned to my brothers, their response was something like: "You know I would love to help out, but my work and family keep my hands full." Besides, my brothers' idea of helping out was to send a check. [March 1984]

Most of these women also supported their families financially during hard times, despite their generally meager wages as domestic workers, laundresses, clerical workers, saleswomen, teachers, social workers, librarians, or nurses. Fourteen of the 50 women supported their parents *completely* for five years or more; another 31 women paid some portion of the living and health costs of their parents. The parents of most of the women had little economic security in old age, and qualified for little or no social security. Their paid work had been done for the most part before 1935, in an era uncovered by social security, or they had been part-time workers, or they had worked inside the home. Only 28 percent of these parents had health insurance during their old age, since the years of care-giving in question were generally before 1965, the start of Medicare and Medicaid coverage. One woman had clear memories of the poverty of her parents in old age:

> My father and mother were savers. They never had much, but they were careful with what they had. At sixty-five, my father's employer, a construction company, made him retire. He had saved up $20,000, a tidy sum for 1941. But then Dad broke his hip and was hospitalized for several months. Mother contracted tuberculosis and needed lots of care for a while. Five years into my father's retirement, his money was gone. [June 1983]

Some of these single women supported their parents before the latter's retirement and old age. In some cases, a parent's extended unemployment required a daughter to help financially. During the Great Depression, 9 of the 50 women found themselves the only member of their immediate family in a paid job. They supported households on their salaries. A clerical worker, whose top salary (earned in 1960, just before her retirement) was $11,580, remembered the years between 1930 and 1936:

> First my father was laid off. Then my brother. They were both bricklayers. My mother had never worked for money. It was 1930, and I was the only one in a job. As a stenographer at Hatchley's, I took home about $17 a week, a pretty good salary for that dismal time.
> We all thought that Dad and Jim would find work within six months. They looked and looked and found nothing. A year went by. Then two. Jim began to drink heavily. Dad kept searching for work. Now and then, he would get a day's wage cleaning someone's house or barn. But after awhile, even he gave up. If the WPA [Work Projects Administration] hadn't come along, Dad might not have worked again. For six years, mine was the only pay we could count on. [February 1982]

Others in this group of women became the sole providers for their households because of a parent's accident at work, disability, or death. A former nurse commented:

> Dad was a tree-trimmer. One day he fell and broke his back. His spine was hurt to such a degree that he never walked again. I was about twenty-eight at the time. From that terrible day on, I supported all three of us until there was only me left. [September 1982]

The emotional and economic resilience exhibited by these never-married women, who supported their families wholly or partially during the Depression or other impoverished times, does not appear to vary with social class. This finding diverges from that of sociologists Glen Elder and Jeffrey Liker, who found, in studying the long-term impact of the Great Depression upon married women and widows who had been young adults during the 1930s, that such adversity, suffered by middle-class women, was linked with confidence, feelings of mastery, and assertiveness in their old age. In contrast, they found that hardships confronted by working-class women appeared to correlate with diminished emotional health and resourcefulness in old age. Regardless of social class, the women I interviewed tended to fit Elder and Liker's model of "self-reliant womanhood [for middle-class women] that is uniquely suited to the living requirements of widowhood."[9]

Why is this so? I suggest three explanations for this cross-class resourcefulness in old age: (1) these women learned self-reliance *in single adulthood* through contending with the financial, physical, occupational, legal, and social demands that the husbands of many married women of the same generations handled; (2) these women chose a never-married path because of self-reliant attributes developed *in childhood and adolescence*; or (3) a combination of adult and childhood socialization developed a flexibility and self-confidence that prepared these women for managing the vicissitudes of both single life and old age.

Under patriarchal capitalism, a man's social class in adulthood is a function of the social class and race of his family of origin, gender, education, occupational and social status, property, consumer credit, and the money he can accrue. A woman's social class is more complicated and contingent. It hinges on all the factors that shape a man's class standing but is mediated additionally by her relationship (or lack thereof) with a husband. For example, most women without a history of full-time paid work who divorce or are widowed—whether working class, middle class, or upper middle class—find that both their income and social class diminish drastically. Conversely, most men who undergo divorce or widowhood have previously established their occupational and credit status, which is little affected by the loss of their wives.

Women who never marry, however, can never share in the social and economic benefits of male privilege. Except for the tiny percentage of those who were born rich, single women are not protected from the imperatives of earning a living, carving out a legitimate social role, and planning for old age. Middle-class and working-class women, alike, who never marry must demonstrate resourcefulness and self-reliance if they are to survive into old age, for both groups are reliant on their own earnings and initiative. Of course, middle-class single women are better able to save or count on a family inheritance than are working-class single women. Single women of middle-class status can build up reserves for middle and old age that their lower-class counterparts cannot. Nonetheless, single status requires of both groups lifelong preparedness and flexibility for facing the contingencies and setbacks of adulthood independently.

We have seen that the families of these women provided support and exacted dutiful responses. In addition, some of the families blocked the women's development, opportunity, and mobility over long periods of time. The conflicts between family wishes and the wishes of some of the never-married women penetrated several dimensions of the latter's lives, such as social reform, paid work, friendship, finances, and travel. The comments of one woman about her family's obstruction of her political participation were similar to those of 7 of the other women:

> I came home from college in 1910 sure that I would work with immigrant orphans. So I told my parents that I was determined to find work or to volunteer in a settlement house in Philadelphia. They at first thought I was joking. Then, when they understood how serious

my commitment was, they urged me to think of my
responsibilities as a daughter and sister. When they saw
that their arguments were not working, they simply for-
bade me to go to a settlement.   [June 1984]

This reminiscence is strikingly similar to a statement of Jane
Addams in the 1890s about middle-class family resistance to the
settlement-house work of their daughters:

They are taught to be self-forgetting and self-sacrificing,
to consider the good of the Whole before the good of
the Ego. But when all this information and culture
show results, when the daughter comes back from college and begins to recognize her social claim to the
"submerged tenth" [the poor], and to evince a disposi-
tion to fill it, the family claim is strenuously asserted;
she is told that she is unjustified, ill-advised in her
efforts. . . . She is restricted and unhappy; her elders,
meanwhile, are unconscious of the situation, and we
have all the elements of a tragedy.[10]

The 7 other women who also reported family interference with
their political activity did so with bitterness, many years after the
intrafamilial battles were waged. One woman's comments are representative:

I was a grown woman when my father vowed that
he would never permit me to campaign for F. D. R.
He thought it was unladylike, and besides he was a
Republican. I did so anyways in 1932. My father
threw me out of the house. We didn't speak again

until 1937, at my mother's fiftieth birthday celebration. [August 1983]

Jobs and careers were another issue before which families of some of the women threw obstacles. Some families objected to a daughter's working at all; other families had distinct views on "acceptable" employment for a single woman. The following remarks, by one of 13 women I interviewed who had faced family opposition to their work interests, were particularly fiery:

> At first my father and brothers said that they would never allow me to work outside our home. My father came from Italy and still thought like a Sicilian head-of-the-house. My brothers imitated him.
>
> So I went on strike. I refused to work, eat, or talk at home. My father beat me and screamed at me. My mother pleaded. Finally, Papa agreed that I could go get a job. So I decided that I wanted to be a nurse. My father was horrified and refused to send me to nursing school, even though at that point he could have afforded it.
>
> At that point, I got a waitress job at a place *not run by an Italian*. My father nearly killed me. So I switched to a restaurant run by a friend of my father. It was then that my father gave up his battle with me about work. I waitressed for awhile and then got a secretarial job, which I liked much more. [September 1982]

Friendships also evoked objection from and, in a few cases, even sabotage by the families of some of the women. Bonds with men elicited parental demands that the women marry or stop the friendship. Friendships with women evoked jealousy and, sometimes, suspicion. One woman encountered family resistance to her relationships with both male and female companions:

> Tom and I went everywhere together. He was my best friend. After a few months of this companionship, my mother called Tom in and asked him his intentions. He said that he intended to be as good a friend to me as I was to him. He also noted that I was twenty-seven, old enough to take care of myself. My mother didn't believe him or me and gave me a hard time every time I wanted to see him.
>
> Tom married a few years later and moved to another town. So he was out of the picture. But, if you can believe it, Mother even objected to my friendship with Jennifer, a woman I worked with. At first, Mother complained that I didn't spend enough time at home. Then she got more specific and said that I spent too much time with Jennifer, that I "was limiting myself." For years I ignored my mother's sniping until she upped the ante and began suggesting that their was something "funny" about Jennifer. When I challenged her about that, she told me that she thought I wasn't spending enough time with men, that she was worried that I was getting "perverted" by Jennifer. It was then that I moved out of Mother's house. [March 1983]

Some families interfered with the women's financial plans as well, and this interference took two forms. Family members, usually parents, insisted that the earnings of the never-married woman be pooled in a family fund that would be disbursed by a parent; or the single woman managed her own funds, but encountered chronic criticism of her expenditures from members of her family. The family's intrusion into one woman's financial affairs elicited this memory:

> In my first job, from 1927 to 1941, I worked a seventy-hour week as a typist and then office manager. On payday, my mother would be waiting at the door to take my paycheck. I never saw a penny of that money. If I wanted lunch money or bus fare, she would give it to me after I explained in detail why I needed it. She treated me as if I were eight years old.
>
> When Mother got senile, do you think I got control over my own wages? Oh no. My aunt, who lived with us, took over the reins then. She was just like Mother, except worse. She kept urging me to take a second job, so the household would not be so up against it. When both she and Mother died, I was forty-six. That was the first time I ever had money of my own to spend. The first thing I did was to take a trip to California. I could just see their fingers waving in heaven (or wherever) at such extravagance. [June 1982]

Travel and other forms of recreation were thwarted by some families of these never-married women, who offered several explanations for familial objection. Some of the women thought their families were hostile to play in general. Others said their families criticized the expenditure of money for other than "necessaries," as one woman put it. Still others suggested that their families did not want them to be influenced by settings other than that of the family. A fourth group of women speculated that their families objected to a woman's playing sports or cards, or going off to sightsee without a husband. One family's attempts to limit the extrafamilial recreation and travel of its never-married member is described here:

> I had never been outside of Philadelphia County, and I was thirty-one. On my birthday, I looked in the mirror and vowed to begin exploring. After all, I worked hard as an emergency room nurse and was a steady contributor to the running of the family home.
>
> So I made a plan to go across Canada by railroad. However, I made the mistake of telling my father and mother. They discouraged me from going, saying that it was too dangerous for a woman alone. But they did not forbid me. The morning I was supposed to leave, my mother came down with some sort of hysterical attack that left her unable to breathe. I could not leave under those circumstances. One week later, I tried to go again, after making elaborate rearrangements at work and with the railroad. Don't you think that Mother again came down with those peculiar attacks? I almost went anyways, but I knew that I would hear for twenty years how I had abandoned my mother in her time of greatest need. [February 1984]

Most of the women's households did *not* constitute prisons, although a few, as can be detected in several of the comments, were close approximations. Usually, the families of these women provided them with a complicated and shifting mix of support, requests for ongoing help, and obstruction. In the light of longstanding stereotypes of the family-bound spinster, of women portrayed as ciphers who eke out joyless, unimaginative lives within archaic family settings, the wealth of variation of family experience reported by these 50 women serves as a necessary corrective.

F O U R / Intimacy

"Our family is the most important thing in the world!" My mother used to say that to me at least three times a day. But I was never sure of that. In fact, after eighty-four years of trying to learn those lines, I've given them up.

Instead I tell people what I really feel—that the ones who hold me up when I stumble are the ones I let into my heart. If they are of my blood, fine. If they aren't, that's fine too.   [January 1984]

Enthronement of the family has made the construction of intimate interdependence among unrelated or unmarried people difficult but, happily, not impossible. Friends outside the family, particularly in Western, industrial, and postindustrial cultures, have proved to be vigorous competitors with relatives throughout the life-course for the attention and loyalty of a family member.[1] Despite the normatively prescribed "inside track" enjoyed by relatives, friends have played as large a role in the emotional and social lives of the women I interviewed as have family members. Indeed, a sizable minority of the women—19 women, or 38 percent—reported that friends eclipsed family members in intimacy and importance to them, once adulthood was reached. Most of these women noted their greater "investment" in friends than in family with guilt, unease, or defensiveness.

Their obvious discomfort in acknowledging their preference for friends over family documents a central point of Michele Barrett and Mary McIntosh, that such a preference constitutes heterodoxy:

> It [the family] is indeed a major agency for caring, but in monopolizing care it has made it harder to undertake other forms of care. It is indeed a unit of sharing, but in demanding sharing within it has made other relations tend to become more mercenary. It is indeed a place of intimacy, but in privileging the intimacy of close kin it has made the outside world cold and friendless, and made it harder to sustain relations of security and trust except with kin. Caring, sharing, and loving would be more widespread if the family did not claim them for its own.[2]

During my interviews, I soon became aware of the central significance of these women's friendships. Photographs of friends were on display in the women's living rooms, and they made many references to friends in response to my questions about work, travel, play, and retirement plans. Although some of the women were uncomfortable discussing the *priority* they assigned friends in their lives, they were uninhibited in detailing the emotional *depth* and *variety* of these relationships.

In reviewing studies of elderly women who had never married, gerontologists Rita Braito and Donna Anderson have speculated that such women might cluster into two categories: the socially isolated and the socially active.[3] With a single exception, the women I interviewed fell into the latter group, perhaps because I did not include institutionalized women in my sample but relied on the referrals of clergy, human service workers, community leaders, students, friends, and the women I was interviewing to find the names of more women to include.

The women I interviewed reported that dyads, two-person bonds, were their most prevalent and most significant form of friendship. According to sociologist George Simmel, dyadic relationships are, for structural reason, the true sites of intimacy. He suggested that the basis of intimacy is the knowledge of participants that a relationship is unique, fragile, and transient. Each member of a dyad realizes his or her indispensability to the relationship and recognizes that a dyad abandoned can never be extended or replaced.[4] Although most of the women's important friendships were dyadic in nature, the majority of these women reported commitment over time to both dyads and group friendships. Most common was a pattern in which a woman sustained a primary, daily, and long-term friendship with one other person, usually another woman, while at the same time joining a circle of two to five other friends at least weekly or twice weekly, either in a group or in pairs. In the second most common pattern, a woman invested exclusively in a strong, dyadic bond. A third friendship constellation was triadic, in which a woman maintained close relationships in a threesome. A few women relied wholly on their family members for social and emotional intimacy, but only one woman reported no close friends or family members.

These relationships were characterized by the three elements that psychologists George Levinger and Harold Raush have identified as constituting authentic intimacy: involvement (personal closeness), commitment, and symmetry (equality of investment in the friendship).[5] The reflections of one woman illustrate all these elements:

> There is nothing I did that Joyce didn't know about. That's 'cause I shared everything with her. She did the same with me. We got to be friends in high school. Then, her Mom died a few years later, so we took an apartment together. We stayed roommates for fifty-seven years, until her heart gave out suddenly six years ago. She just dropped dead in front of me one night. I'm still reeling from that loss. She leaned on me all those years just like I relied on her. In selfish moments, I wish that I had gone before her. Now I come home to silence and to memories.   [June 1984]

Fifty-seven years of sharing a residence is a long time, but not necessarily unusual. Long-lived, committed friendship was one the most common elements of these women's lives; yet they were willing to create new relationships at various points of their lifecourse, including old age. As a consequence, their biographies teem with short-, middle-, and long-term bonds, as Table 4 suggests.

TABLE 4 / Relative Duration of Friendships

Total in Friendship Constellation	No. of Friendships with Women	Duration in Years
39 primary dyads (daily contact)	4	1–10
	4	11–20
	7	21–30
	8	31–40
	5	41–50
	6	51–60
	2	61–70
	3	71–80
4 primary triads (daily contact)	2	1–10
	4	11–20
	2	21–30
5 additional primary dyads that resulted from dissolution of triads (daily contact)	2	1–10
	4	11–20
	2	21–30
98 secondary friendships from groups of 2 to 5 friends (weekly or twice-weekly contact)	19	1–10
	21	11–20
	25	21–30
	13	31–40
	11	41–50
	9	51–60

To understand intimacy among never-married old women, it is important to examine not only the duration of their friendships but also the roles that friendship plays at each portion their life cycle, especially since these women violated the life-cycle norms of marriage and childraising. The period between the ages of eighteen and thirty was a time of exploration and decision-making about work, marriage, and childbearing for most of the 50 women. In these years, during which familial and social pressures to marry increased and peaked, most of the women I interviewed reported that their female friends were their chief source of validation and companionship. Most of these women were dating men and carefully weighing the prospective costs and benefits of marrying:

> In my early twenties, my girl friends and I checked out LIFE. We dated men, worked our first jobs, chose careers, and tried to figure out what we wanted. Most of us wanted marriage and kids. By the time I was twenty-five, most girls were married or spending most of their time trying to get that way. I learned a great deal about myself through conversations with those girls. Most importantly, I learned that my way would have to be different. The things my girl friends did to get a man didn't interest me. Some even alarmed me. Can you imagine a capable girl "playing dumb" with her beau or faking helplessness?
>
> At about age twenty-eight, I knew I faced a serious choice. If I did not take one of the offers coming my way from the sweet but uninspiring men I dated, I would soon be left high and dry. So, with the help of my friends, both married and single, I made that choice. I took a look around me at who I wanted to spend time with over the next fifty to sixty years. It wasn't any of the men who courted me. It was the girls I spent time with who, like me, were reluctant to become what a wife was expected to be in 1935. [September 1983]

These women also looked to friends for good times and intimacy. The sharp contrast between the ease of friendship and the anxieties of courtship, experienced by one of the women when she was in her twenties, was documented in the stories of 27 other women as well:

> I could never quite understand why I felt so good about myself with my girl friends and so at odds with myself when I was with men I was seeing. Now, I dated *good* men and ones with whom I had plenty in common. Yet somehow other people's expectations came crowding in when I was with them. With the girls, I could just be me. With the men, I had to somehow be fitting into a mold of "potential wife and mother." Four men waited around for me to agree to marry them. Each time I thought long and hard about the fact that as much as I liked Joe or Harry or Edward or John, I preferred my life with the girls. I never put it quite like that as it sounded rather strange. But at eighty-one I feel free to tell the truth—that I liked much more to be with female companions who took me as I was than to be with men who were taught to size me up as poten- tial. [May 1984]

In the decade between ages thirty and forty, these women braved, for the first time, the status of "old maid." During these first years past the optimal age of marriageability, they developed lasting bonds with other women who had also decided to sail against the prevailing winds. Friendships with other single women proved to be the most significant and frequent extrafamilial invest- ment of the women I interviewed. Indeed, their friendship with people much like themselves in age, gender, and marital status is congruent with the tendency Robert Bell found among adults of all marital statuses: they develop circles of friends who are "highly homogeneous" in social and demographic characteristics, as well as in interests and values.[6]

> Most of my friends back then were other schoolteachers I knew from work. We had so much in common, including the odd business of contending with other people's judgments about us being "old maids." It was just natural to spend time with other women who understood the demands of a life in which one had to make a living, take care of parents, and maintain an independent and dignified existence at the same time, all in the face of foolish stereotypes. [June 1984]

However, these women also created and sustained important bonds with married, divorced, and widowed women who looked to same-sex friendship for comradeship. In their thirties, the women whom I interviewed had also developed friendships with married and single men who sought out their companionship:

> Bert and I played chess together two nights a week for more than thirty years. We also talked shop a lot, "shop" being ideas about how children learn and how to incorporate theories about learning into our teaching.
>
> The only thing I felt uneasy about with Bert was his way of talking about his problems with his marriage. So I would stop him each time and remark that he should work such matters out with his wife or with a counselor. You see, I felt compromised as a woman by his complaints about his wife. He would stop and then say: "Hilda, you're the best friend I have in the world. Why didn't I marry you when I had the chance?" I would

answer: "Bert, you were always much too important to me to relegate to the marriage heap." He never quite understood that. [June 1983]

In middle and late middle age, these women solidified and deepened their friendships and involved their closest friends in planning for life after retirement. Some friends from childhood, adolescence, college, and work, as well as some of their traveling companions from their years between ages forty and sixty-five, proved to be tried and tested allies, whose character, habits, and idiosyncracies were well known and liked. One woman's reflections on friendship in her middle years represent the statements of many:

Maureen and I met in nursing school. We kept up with our friendship through our first jobs, through many courtships, and on into our thirties. We found ourselves by coincidence working together at Lady of Mercy Hospital right after the war. That led us to get a house together in 1947. Since then we've been like hand and glove. We took all our vacations together and used them to travel all over the world. Her friends were mine and vice versa.

When I reached fifty-five, I began to think about retirement. I tried to convince Maureen to enroll in the same retirement community as me for whenever we got too old to be in our house. I certainly thought it would be more comforting and fun to do that with her than without her. She took a year to think about it and then agreed. We moved here to this community together five years ago. But six months after we arrived, she came down with brain cancer, which took her within eight months. I was numb for almost a year after she died. She was everything to me. [September 1982]

The pervasiveness of this woman's bond with Maureen is typical of the primary relationships many women remembered from middle age. They invested heavily in such relationships and from them derived long-term companionship and support. In addition, these women relied on friends for emotional and logistical sustenance in providing care for their aging parents. For nearly all the women (42 of 50), care-giving became a central priority in their late forties and fifties, when their parents became physically and economically dependent upon them. They turned to friends for solace, advice, and time off, as in this account:

> Mother lost the use of her legs when I was just starting work at Dottle High. We could not afford daytime help, so I would race home at lunch to feed her. At night, Nancy would come over to spend time with us. She was always a great favorite of Mother's as well as of mine. So her nightly visits became the highlight of our evening. Nancy would take shifts now and then to give me a night out. Sometimes she would give Mother lunch when I couldn't get away. Most of all, she was there, year in and year out, to remind me of life outside the toil of bedpans and to lighten up the crushing exhaustion that comes with taking care of a parent. When Mother got bad, Nancy talked to me for a year and a half about putting her in a home. I wouldn't listen at first. But Nancy persisted. She took me to some to show me they were not all ghastly. I finally agreed when Mother became incoherent. Nancy went with me to put Mother in the home and came with me twice a week on visits. *That* is friendship. [May 1983]

As the workplace declined or disappeared as a source of challenge and companionship, friendships, like family relations, increased in importance for these single women as they moved into retirement. The high priority they assigned to friendship throughout their life-course resulted in their later years in close companions who had known them in a wide range of contexts. As a consequence, only 7 of the 50 women had no regular contact with a long-term, intimate friend at the time of the interview. Of these 7, 6 had chosen to rely on family members rather than friends throughout their adult lives; one relied on no one as an adult. Forty-three of the women (86 percent) identified at least one close friend with whom she had at least twice-weekly contact. Fifteen women (30 percent) lived with a friend for five years or more after age sixty-five, sharing a room, an apartment, a home, or a residence in a retirement community or private home. One woman's comments, which illustrate the interdependency with friends during retirement, were similar to those reported by the great majority of the 50:

> Polly, my buddy since grammar school, died in May of 1978. I was sick with sorrow for months and months. So I started to make myself go to a senior citizen center in the neighborhood on a daily basis to try to reduce my loneliness. Soon after I joined up, I met two girls who have become real friends to me even outside the center. We take trips together, go shopping for each other, and, most important, talk every evening about troubles we're having or things that are on our mind. They listen, they really listen to me each time. They make me feel like an important person in the same way that Polly used to. [May 1982]

Exploring friendships among never-married old women across their life cycle, I found few differences in the depth, duration, and variety of the friendships among middle-class and working-class women. There was, however, a greater tendency among the working-class women to rely more often on family members than on friends for assistance in old age, but I found evidence of this class difference only in the retirement years. Perhaps the closer proximity of working-class women to their extended families made them more likely than middle-class women to choose kin over kith in times of reduced mobility and greatest need.

Regardless of their social class, ascribed or achieved, the large majority of women constructed lives in which same-sex friendships predominated.[7] As Table 5 indicates, 82 percent of all the significant relationships identified by these 50 women were with other women.

Same-sex friendships predominated for several reasons. Most of the women I interviewed were employed in sex-segregated occupations, such as clerical work, domestic work, nursing, teaching, and social work; therefore, friends derived from work settings would probably be women. Besides, most of the women said they found women easier to confide in than men because of women's capacities for empathic listening and nurturance. The women also reported that their lives, past and present, were much more like the lives of other women than of the men of their acquaintance. Additionally, 14 women explained that close friendship with men usually led to sexual advances, whereas close relationships with women did not. Finally, 23 women said they had encountered a cultural taboo against single women forming closing bonds with married men. (Since fewer than 10 percent of the men born into the same birth cohorts as these women remained unmarried past the age of forty, the women with whom I spoke had usually met married men—at work, in the neighborhoods, and in the various groups to which they belonged.[8]) Like the woman whose comments follow, these women generally found same-sex relationships easier to create, maintain, and enjoy than cross-sex friendships.

TABLE 5 / Gender Patterns of Friendship

Total in	No. of Friendships	
Friendship Constellation	with Women	with Men
39 primary dyads (daily contact)	35	4
4 primary triads (daily contact)	6	2
98 secondary friendships in circles of 2 to 5 friends (weekly or twice-weekly contact)	78	20

Guys have always been in my life, but more as buddies to joke with than friends to lean on. I think that is so because I have usually found that men want you to pay inordinate amounts of attention to them. Or they want to go to bed with you the minute things get friendly. I have not found either of these difficulties with women. Also, women don't usually need to be in charge of a friendship. They just swim with it wherever it takes them. If I sound prejudiced, so be it. Women have simply "been there for me" in lots of ways men have not. [March 1982]

The "Boston marriage," a nineteenth-century phrase for a long-term, exclusive emotional commitment between two never-married women who share a household over many years, characterized the lives of 14 of these 50 women. Of these 14, 7 women had lived with a friend since their meeting in college, nursing school, or normal school; 3 women had shared an apartment or house with a friend from their mid-twenties; and 4 of the women had jointly owned or rented a house with a friend from the time they were in their thirties or forties. The depth and breadth of the interdependency in these 14 relationships appeared to match the longevity of these bonds, judging from the following account:

> Roberta and I met on my first job. I was a clerk-typist then and a mere slip of a girl of eighteen. I was living at home and trying to save enough money to get my own place.
>
> Roberta was a worldly twenty-two and had been on her own since sixteen. She saw that I was scared to death and helped me out in any way she could. After six months of lunch hours with her, I could tell that she would be easy to live with and full of fun. So I elected to move into her apartment and share expenses.
>
> That was sixty-one years ago. Thanks to our mutual good health, we're still here, sharing the same address. We've seen three continents together, lost all our parents together, pooled our money and assets for more than fifty years, and shared every friend either of us has ever had. I rely on her in every imaginable way. But, happily, that's a two-way street, so it works out fine. God knows we've had our spats, but none that we could not resolve with a bit of trying.   [August 1984]

Although the content of this woman's narrative was unexceptional among the 14 women who sustained such a long-term and central relationship, its direct and nondefensive form was unusual. More commonly, women who had lived in "Boston marriages" answered, or evaded, questions about their intimate relationships in a self-protective manner. Their elliptical, sometimes cryptic form of response lends credence to Lillian Faderman's thesis that Freudianism has cast lasting shadows over the social acceptability of single women carving out lives together.[9]

Never-married women born just two generations earlier, in the 1850s and 1860s, had shared households, incomes, and friendships over a lifetime without evoking suspicions of "perversion" or lesbianism. They were able to do so because of the widespread nineteenth-century conviction about women's "passionlessness," a cluster of beliefs about the poverty of women's carnal nature and the comparative richness of their spiritual capacities.[10] By the early twentieth century, however, belief in women's "passionlessness" had been supplanted by notions of the omnipresence of libido. Somewhat earlier, between 1884 and 1886, historian Carroll Smith-Rosenberg has determined, the term "lesbianism" had entered the public domain.[11] Accordingly, these comments exemplify the defensive attitude of 8 of the 14 women who had been part of a "Boston marriage":

> We have shared a home for a long time now. I suppose you'll want to make much of that. But don't. These forty-odd years together have been as aboveboard and regular as can be. I wished I had lived in a time in which people didn't impose their own imaginings on innocent friendship. Not everyone, after all, is full of lurid cravings. Some of us just live simply and mind our own business. [January 1984]

Although some of the women *did* "live simply and mind [their] own business," others chose to introduce erotic elements into their lives. Unfortunately, it is impossible to know how many women took female lovers, because of the face-to-face interviewing method I employed. As I learned early in my research, very few of these old, single women were willing to entertain questions about their sexual history. Fewer still agreed to answer such questions. As one of the women declared, after I asked if she were willing to discuss her intimate friendships: "Young woman, you have gone past the boundaries of proper behavior. To ask such a question is to show deplorable disrespect to me in my own home after I have graciously received you. You must leave now."

Leave I did—but I initiated questions about sexual activity two more times. Each time, I was similarly rebuffed, and immediately lost rapport with the woman with whom I was speaking—and rapport is the *sine qua non* of successful interviewing. Consequently, I no longer initiated questions about intimate or sexual pasts and presents. Instead, I waited for a cue from each woman (implicit or explicit) that signified her willingness to discuss sexual intimacy *before* I posed such questions. Only 9 of the 50 women (18 percent) indicated such openness, so that the refusal or reluctance of the other 41 women (82 percent) suggests the pervasive attitude against sensuality (or the impropriety of discussing sex or sensuality) of women born between 1884 and 1918 in the United States.

The unwillingness of 82 percent of the women to discuss sex and sexuality may also indicate their *resistance* to collaborating with investigatory processes that Michel Foucault has characterized as part of the "policing of sex," a process of "regulating sex through useful and public discourses."[12]

As a group of violators of the marriage norm, the 41 women who did not speak about their own sexual histories might well have perceived that their self-interest required a *refusal* to open their lives to public discourse. Their refusal may have been political in nature or, perhaps, it may have constituted a moral preference for keeping sexual details private.

The 9 women who were willing to discuss their intimate histories asserted strong preferences for long-term sexual relationships. Four of these women had engaged in short-term sexual bonds before settling into long-term commitments. Five of the 9 women discussed a heterosexual experience, 3 women reported lesbian relationships, and one woman described a life of celibacy. None of them spoke of sexual experience with both sexes.

Family members, schoolmates, colleagues from work and voluntary organizations, and roommates proved significant to these women; neighbors, by contrast, did not during most of the women's adulthood. Generally, they reported casual, episodic, and distant contact with neighbors. Many suggested that their work lives, friendships, and family commitments had left them little time for much else. One woman's reflections on her lack of investment in neighbors were characteristic of the group as a whole:

> In a relaxed way, I "knew" my neighbors. I chatted over the fence once a week when I mowed the lawn, and I loaned that cup of sugar whenever anybody needed it. But I never knew my neighbors like my mother had. I was much too busy bringing in the family's only income and managing the household, once Mother no longer could.
>
> Mother, by contrast, had a best friend across the street for fifty years who was in and out of our house all the time. Why, those two raised their families together and were like sisters to each other. *That* sort of friendship I made elsewhere—on the job and at my church. [January 1983]

Yet, during three special times of their lives—in youth, old age, and crises—the women I interviewed *did* cultivate intimate bonds with their neighbors. Moreover, this selective pattern of investment in neighbors does not appear to be particular to single women. In her studies of friendship among people of all marital statuses, sociologist Beth Hess has found that neighborhood friendships are taken most seriously by the very young and the very old.[13] For people who are undergoing periods of special vulnerability and limited mobility, neighbors may become uniquely accessible companions and helpers. Indeed, during childhood, old age, and crises, one's capacity to search for solace and assistance is most restricted at the very time that one's need for comradeship and help is greatest.

The following remarks, by three women, illustrate the range of contexts in which neighbors were transformed into friends. The first woman spoke about a friend she had made in childhood:

> Joan and I began walking to and from school together in first grade. It took no time at all for us to realize that we had a terrible problem in common—a parent who was a drunk. I figured it out during the second or third week of school when I picked Joan up and found her father on the floor in the kitchen. Joan, in turn, took no time at all to discover that my ever-present black and blue marks came from my mother on her "mornings after." We spent our childhood helping each other get through. By the time we graduated from high school, we were lifelong buddies. We went to nursing school together and have remained the closest of companions to this day. [June 1982]

Another woman's thoughts on a friendship she had made with a neighbor during retirement are representative:

> Molly had just lost her dearest friend. So had I, two years earlier. When we met six years ago in the laundromat, it took very little time to learn that we were two

very old ladies in a highly similar situation. We were
both survivors of lots of once-living and now-dead companions. Her humor and generosity drew me toward
her immediately. She, meanwhile, seemed to think that I
was the most interesting eighty-five-year-old she had
met in years. Approximately one year into our friendship, we combined our money and took an apartment
together. That will remain our arrangement until one of
us kicks the bucket or gets too senile to know that there
is a bucket to kick. [August 1984]

All three women found friends among their neighbors during
the illnesses and deaths of parents, during their own illnesses and
accidents, and while mourning for their dead or dying friends. The
third woman told me:

One day I came home from work to find Father lying at
the foot of the stairs. He had blacked out on his way up
or down. I called an ambulance and then Phyllis from
across the street, because I had noticed her car parked
on the block when I arrived. In my panic, I called her,
even though I didn't know her very well, since she had
only lived on the block for a little more than a year.
She was the greatest help to us in that terrible time.
She insisted on doing all sorts of things for Father. This
mere acquaintance became my best friend within the
year, because of her splendid availability to Father and
her endless willingness to give to me. [May 1983]

Of the total 145 primary and secondary friendships of these 50
women, 5 of their primary friends and 11 secondary friends (those
seen weekly or twice weekly, usually in a group) were neighbors

when the friendships were cemented. Thus neighbors constituted just over 10 percent of the most significant bonds and the
next most intimate (secondary) relationships for the women I
interviewed.

Unquestionably, the chief source of friendship for these never-
married old women was their workplace. (All but one of the 50
women had worked full-time for at least thirty years.) These
women, of course, spent a large proportion of their waking hours
during adulthood at work, and one of them expressed the value of
her fellow workers this way:

> You cannot work at a place for thirty-one years without
> becoming immensely familiar with the people around
> you. I found that I looked forward eagerly each morn-
> ing to that coffee break with the girls. They made me
> laugh and taught me about parts of the world I had not
> yet seen myself. Coffee breaks led to lunches. Lunches
> led to dinners. Dinners led to friendship.
>
> Sybil, Joy, and I have been fast friends for more than
> twenty years. It all started at work and spread out from
> there. We've lived together, vacationed together, and now
> have even retired together. And all thanks to the coffee
> breaks at Popper and Sons, Inc. [February 1983]

Collegial relationships, formed at work, constituted the largest
network of friends. Next in number were friendships formed in
volunteer church work, with service groups, or in political organizations. High school, college, and graduate school were other important sources of friends. Table 6 shows the locales in which these
women made friends.

The women I studied proved to be socially engaged persons,
individuals whose "self-portraits" located friends and friendship at

TABLE 6 / Derivations of Friendships

Total in Friendship Constellation	Work	Volunteer Activity			High School, College, or Professional School	Neighborhood
		Church	Service	Political		
47 dyads or triads (daily contact)	19	5	7	3	8	5
98 secondary friendships in groups of 2 to 5 (weekly or twice-weekly contact)	50	11	10	7	9	11
145 primary and secondary friendships	69	16	17	10	17	16

the heart of their everyday life. Their lives are not characterized by the severe loneliness that sociologist Robert Weiss finds prevalent among unmarried people.[14] Probably, therefore, there are two significant groups of old, single women: the socially active and the socially isolated. Given the stereotypes that characterize never-married women as lonely old maids, it is important to recognize that the lives of many never-married women are rich with friends and intimates.

One emerges from compiling these accounts of never-married old women's intimate bonds with a sharpened sense of the diverse ways they have found for building support, companionship, security, emotional and sexual intimacy, intergenerational links, and community into their lives. Our imagination—impoverished, as

Martha Ackelsberg has noted, by a vocabulary that has very limited reference to alternatives to the nuclear-family model—is enriched by these women's example.[15] This group of never-married women expands our capacity to articulate and picture varied social relations with kin and non-kin. By so doing, they extend our realization and, eventually, legitimation of plural paths to intimacy. They thereby help to undermine the political and ideological supremacy of the nuclear family, a supremacy that isolates many within the family, makes deviants out of those who never marry, and provides structural reinforcements for male domination.

A parallel inference that surfaces in exploring these never-married women's friendships is that heterosexism—the privileging of heterosexual relations over celibacy, bisexuality, or homosexuality—continues to stigmatize and denigrate old, single women because they have not exhibited sufficiently clear proof of their heterosexuality. The women I interviewed have lived most of their lives under suspicion of arrested development or perversion, and "compulsory heterosexuality" (Adrienne Rich's memorable term) has required these never-married women to justify their status, to explain their assumed manlessness, to prove their womanliness, to account for their childlessness, and, in general, to defend their normality.[16] Such enforced defensiveness is draining and constraining. This challenge has not, however, defeated this group of women. Instead, they have constructed their lives on their own terms, against strong odds.

FIVE / Work

I was the chief stenographer at Brown's Masonry for forty-three years. The pay was poor. The work was repetitive most of the time. But I knew I was indispensable there, and they knew it too. I had the minute-by-minute history of that company in my brain. The very files were my creation. Why, when the people came in to computerize our office, they had to ask me to for all the details about the last ten years of billing and accounts-payable procedures that Brown's had established.

In return, those computer guys taught me how to "access" information and create files on their new gadgets. I loved the computers they brought in. I would have stayed on another ten years if not for the mandatory retirement age of seventy.   [December 1983]

Whether domestic workers, factory workers, clerical workers, sales people, professionals, or managers, most of the women I interviewed emphasized three themes in their work life: (1) how badly they had been paid; (2) how few were the choices of occupation open to them when they were young, searching for first jobs and training; and (3) how central to their identity working for pay has proved to be. While reporting on the dehumanizing dimensions of work, they also noted the joy and dignity that working had provided.

For the 20 professional and managerial women in my sample, the work itself was challenging. Most of those in more routinized pursuits found the jobs, *per se*, dull, nevertheless, they enjoyed earning money and performing an essential task, no matter how routine. They liked the rhythms of the job and the camaraderie at the workplace. A former worker in a perfume manufacturing plant remarked:

> I worked because I had to, and I worked because I wanted to. I had to work to keep bread on the table and to take care of Mother. I wanted to work because I looked forward to seeing the women on the line with me everyday. They became like family to me. I've always wanted to know lots of people. An assembly line is one way to find them.   [June 1982]

Another woman, a former secretary, also highlighted the sociality that work provided:

> If I had stayed at home all those years, I would have become a nut case. All my life I've been one to get out

of the house every morning. On Saturday, I work with the Girl Scouts. On Sunday, I go to church. Even if I could have earned my keep at home, I wouldn't have wanted to. Walking to work, chatting with the neighbors, buying a few groceries, having lunch with a buddy are all part of normal life to me. Without that, I would have felt cooped up, like an invalid. [March 1984]

A woman who had worked as a stenographer and then as an administrative assistant commented on the contrast between the seemingly boundless nature of her housework and the much easier, and more enjoyable, eight-hour workday:

When I do housework, I notice that there are no clear starts or stops. There's always cooking or cleaning or laundering to do. Letters to write, clothes to mend, relatives to call. But when I went to work, it was all much clearer. The tasks were specific, The boss set priorities, and the workday was eight hours long, period. Then, again, I never got lonely at work. The other girls kept me laughing at Roger's for all those forty-eight years. How I miss them. [January 1984]

Work posed problems as well as opportunities to the women. Low pay was their most common complaint. The women felt underpaid in two senses: they believed they were paid less than men who performed identical or similar work, and that the kinds of jobs they performed were undervalued by society. In addition, most of the women remembered few opportunities for advancement. A retired worker, from a hat-making plant, commented on her pay and mobility in relation to her male peers:

> I started on the line at Boch's in 1931 at the rate of $6.50 a week. Right in the heart of the Depression. Everybody told me that I was lucky to even find a job. Seven months later, two guys started at $12.75 a week, doing exactly the same work I was doing. In fact, I was told to teach the men how to do their bit on the hat rims. Within the year, both of the guys were moved to better-paying jobs. Now, nobody offered me the opportunity to move up. The same for the other girls on the line. We just watched the men move past us year after year. The true rub came when one man I trained was made foreman over us. That burned bad. He was a very nice guy, but it's hard to stomach being passed over and underpaid just because you're a woman. [March 1983]

A former domestic worker reflected on her wage history and on the low value assigned to her work and to black people by society:

> I always did a full day's work, but I never got a full day's pay. In the 1930s, when I began cleaning other people's houses, I got twenty-five cents for a day's work. Forty years later, I made twenty dollars a day for scrubbing, cooking, laundering, and ironing. That's better, but still lousy pay. Nobody seems to think that keeping a house nice is worth anything. That's why black folks still get stuck with the broom and the iron. [January 1983]

Women's complaints of low pay are substantiated by U. S. government statistics on wages and salaries paid to women during the twentieth century. Year-round, full-time working women, who were white, earned between 51.4 and 65.5 percent of what white men earned between 1939 and 1984. "Women of color" earned less than a fourth (23.0 percent) of white men's median income in 1939. By 1984, minority women who work full-time were earning only 60.0 percent of the median income earned by white men in that year. Throughout the period from 1939 to 1984, minority women earned substantially lower wages and salaries than white women, though the disparity decreased over time. In 1939, minority women earned only 37.9 percent of white women's median earnings. By 1984, minority women made 91.6 percent of white women's salaries.[1]

How do the earnings of the never-married women I spoke with compare with these statistics? Of the 50 women interviewed, 43 volunteered information on their peak wages or salary for full-time, year-round work before retirement (see Table 7). (Seven women could not remember, or appeared reluctant to discuss, the specifics of their earnings.) As Table 7 shows, the peak salaries or wages of these never-married women cluster in the lower range of the earnings continuum. In interpreting these figures, it must be remembered that 31 of the 43 women who reported earnings made their peak earnings before 1970, in which year $5,323 was the median wage or salary for women working year-round and full-time in the United States.[2]

These low peak salaries and wages reflect, in part, the low median earnings of workers of earlier eras. However, the never-married women's low salaries and wages document the discrimination by gender and, in the case of minority women, by race. The low peak earnings also reflect the sex segregation in the workplace (which has remained at virtually the same level in the

TABLE 7 / Earnings of Never-Married
Women Working Full-Time, Year-Round

Peak Annual Earnings	Number of Women
$3,000–$5,000	10
5,001– 7,000	11
7,001–10,000	8
10,001–15,000	5
15,001–20,000	3
20,001–30,000	3
30,001–40,000	2
40,001–50,000	1

Note: This table is based on the women who reported income.

United States since 1900).[3] One woman, a retired bookkeeper, commented on wage discrimination and sex segregation at work:

> The boss used to make speeches about how well he paid the breadwinners on his payroll. I was one of them, though he seemed to ignore that fact. You see, he thought that only men lived on the salaries they earned . . .
> One side of the office was the "Bookkeeping Section." The other side was known as the "Accounting Section." We all did the same work, except women were in one, and men were in the other. Guess who made the living wage? The men all made twice my salary, at minimum. I know because I was in charge of the payroll for forty-two years. [February 1984]

Historian Alice Kessler-Harris has estimated that "overall, between 1910 and 1940, from 86–90% of all women worked in only 10 different occupations—an occupational concentration that contributed to the ability to assign low wages and poor status to these jobs."[4]

Even in 1969, half of all working women were employed in just 21 of the 250 occupations surveyed by the Bureau of the Census. By contrast, half of all working men were distributed in 65 occupations in that year. One-fourth of all employed women in the United States worked in one of five jobs: secretary-stenographer, household worker, bookkeeper, elementary schoolteacher, or waitress.[5]

Furthermore, most women workers throughout the twentieth century have worked in predominantly "female jobs," jobs in which 70 percent or more of the workers are women. In 1900, 55 percent of U.S. women worked in female-dominated occupations; in 1960, 52 percent of U.S. women still did.[6] A schoolteacher remembered her efforts to move into an occupational stratum generally reserved for men during her working years:

> After completing fourteen years of teaching, receiving three district-wide teaching awards, and obtaining a unanimous petition of endorsement from the other teachers at my school, I applied for a job as an elementary school principal. The district superintendent just laughed at me when I first met with him to discuss the possibility. Then he grew annoyed when I kept calling him to find out my chances. After the fourth or fifth year of applying for a principalship, I got called in to see him.
>
> He said to me: "Miss Nelligan, we have excised your name from present and future eligibility for a principal's position."

"Why?" I asked.

"You have not demonstrated sufficient leadership potential," he responded.

"And I suppose Sherman, Harrigan, and Oaks had done so before you kicked them upstairs?" I asked angrily. (Sherman, Harrigan, and Oaks were three physical education teachers in my school, all men, who had been made principals, one after the other, within their first eight years of teaching.)

"Indeed, they did, Miss Nelligan. As you know, it is most unprofessional for you to cast aspersions in this manner. That is precisely the sort of behavior that prevents you from being taken seriously as administrative timber," he lectured me.

I stormed out of his office then and reflected years after on the forest of incompetents he had promoted over me and others like me.   [March 1982]

According to sociologist Patricia Roos, this teacher's inability to break out of the confines of women's occupational strata and jobs is in line with the prevailing pattern in the contemporary United States and in the eleven other industrialized countries she studied.

Roos found that between 1974 and 1977 in the United States, 33.2 percent of women performed clerical or clerically-related jobs, and 19.2 percent of women performed service work. In short, 52.4 percent of all U.S. working women, held either clerical or service jobs in the mid-1970s. Roos concludes that women remain clustered in relatively few occupations, occupations that are still highly segregated by gender.[7]

For women of color in the United States, "occupational ghettoization" during the twentieth century has been extreme. Jacqueline Jones has documented that, in the first four decades of the twentieth century, black women were predominantly agricultural laborers in rural settings and domestic workers in urban settings. During the 1930s, 9 out of 10 black women workers were agricultural or domestic laborers.[8]

By 1940, only 1.3 percent of all black women who worked for wages had clerical jobs, compared with 33 percent of white women. In that same year, 60 percent of all black working women were domestic servants compared to only 10 percent of white women. A decade later, in 1950, 60 percent of all black female workers in the United States were employed in service jobs in private homes or institutions; 16 percent of all white working women were in service jobs. Only 5 percent of all black women workers held clerical or sales positions in 1950, compared with 40 percent of all white working women.[9] With outright bitterness, a black woman described her attempts to become a saleswoman at a well-known Philadelphia department store:

> In 1952, I celebrated my fortieth birthday and vowed to myself that I would find some work different from the housework I had done since I was fourteen. After all, I had a high school degree and a good head on my shoulders.
>
> So I went down to Law's Department Store and filled out some papers for a sales position. I didn't hear, and I didn't hear. So I went back down to see what was going on. You see, they had ads each week in the newspaper that kept saying they needed sales help.
>
> "Oh no, Miss, we don't need any more help," they told me. Two weeks later, the personnel manager called me to ask if I would join their maintenance staff. I got the message loud and clear and never went back to that store for a job, or for any other reason, either. [May 1984]

Among never-married women workers in the United States of *all* races, segregation by gender has been conspicuous. Roos has found that though never-married women's occupational distribution is somewhat different from that of *ever*-married women in the United States, both sets of women remain in female-dominated categories. Never-married women are more likely than ever-married women to work in high-prestige clerical and service employment and in low-prestige professions. Thus women in the United States, if they remain single, tend to work in jobs that have significantly higher prestige, though *not* higher wage scales, than do ever-married women.[10]

> On the whole, they [the data] suggest that never-married women are more like men in their labor-force behavior, in the sense that they are more likely than married women to participate in the labor force, and to work full time when they are employed. At the same time, however, despite their greater labor-force commitment, never-married women are concentrated in very different jobs from those in which men are employed, working in clerical jobs and the female professions rather than in higher-paying male employment. . . . The female professions do not differ very much in prestige, or average pay, from the kinds of jobs in which married women are employed—clerical, sales, and service work. Thus, although marital responsibilities affect the kinds of jobs in which women work, these differences are not large and for the most part do not translate into differences in prestige or wage rate.[11]

The work patterns of the 50 women I interviewed support these generalizations, and their occupational distribution is shown in Table 8.

TABLE 8 / Occupations of 50
Never-Married Women

Occupation	Number
Domestic worker	6
Factory worker	8
Candy	2
Hats	1
Perfume	2
Women's undergarments	3
Retail salesperson	2
Women's clothes	1
Purses	1
Lab technician	1
Clerical worker	13
Administrative and executive assistant	5
Typist, stenographer, bookkeeper	8
Professional	17
College professor*	2
Physician*	1
Accountant*	1
Social worker	4
Nurse	3
Librarian	2
Teacher	4
Manager	3
Radio-television*	1
Insurance*	1
Pharmaceutical*	1

*Indicates woman worker in an occupation in which women were in the minority between 1930 and 1970.

Only 7 of the 50 women (14 percent) were employed in non-traditional women's work, and each of the 50 women, including the 7 in nontraditional jobs, noted the scarcity of jobs, trades, and careers open to women throughout their working lives. In addition, they commented on the absence of role models in other than "women's work." They also discussed their socialization, pertaining to "appropriate" and feasible work for women, within their families, schools, churches, and neighborhoods. One woman, who had worked as an assistant to a hospital administrator for fifty-four years, said:

> I graduated from high school the year President Wilson was first elected, in 1913. There were exactly five choices open to me then. I could get married, or I could become a secretary, factory worker, waitress, or book-keeper. My family and I had no money to send me to college, so schoolteaching was out of the question, and night classes at normal school were not then available. Even cleaning houses was out of the question, since only Irish and black girls did that then. And no girls I knew thought about starting their own businesses in 1913. Where would we have found the initial capital? Or the customers?
>
> Nowadays, young girls *can* go into business. Were I twenty-five years old now, I would start my own dress shop and make it into something. But in 1913, girls just took orders while men took the risks.   [August 1983]

All but one of the 50 women worked full-time, and continuously, between their first job and their retirement. (By "continuously," I mean that they stayed in one job or firm all their worklife or, if they lost or changed jobs, took another position within two months of leaving the preceding job.) Twenty-two of the 50 women worked part-time after retiring.

Above all else, work meant economic survival. (The only exception was the woman who knew she would inherit a substantial fortune upon the death of her aged mother.) Most of the women had no intention or plan of marrying and, consequently, no hope of someday substituting marriage for work. (White women who married simply disappeared from the workforce during the years in which these 50 women were formulating conceptions of work and women's roles, but black women were much more likely to remain in the paid labor force after marriage. Fewer than 10 percent of white women in the U.S. labor market between 1870 and 1920 were married, according to historian Claudia Goldin.)[12] For these never-married women, as for most men of their generations, employment was an economic necessity.

One woman remembered the importance of her first job:

> I came to Philadelphia from a small town in upstate Pennsylvania at age sixteen. My family's farm had gone under a few years before, and I knew that I would be a drain on the family if I stayed any longer in Laurel County with them, where there was no work to be found for a girl of my age.
>
> I came with enough money to last five days. After that, it was strictly up to me. The stakes were stark and clear. If I could not find work quickly and make a living wage, I could not eat or buy shelter. What sharp spurs hunger and cold are to finding work! It only took me two days to find a job that I kept for the next thirteen years. I came to the city financially desperate and thought myself to be in that state for a long time after that was actually the case.   [March 1983]

Paid work also meant economic independence. Employment obviated the need to rely on parents, siblings, extended family, or friends for money. Economic self-reliance, in turn, purchased social autonomy. If a single woman could pay her own way, no matter how marginally, she could afford to make choices about her life that might be at odds with those that her family or friends preferred. One woman spoke explicitly about the link between economic independence and social and emotional liberty:

> Though I lived with Mama until her death, when I was sixty-three, I was reliant on *only* my own wages and benefits all those years. To have relied on her for money would not only have been grossly unfair to her in her middle and old age, but also would have been dreadful for me. After all, a grown woman should be able to take care of herself.
>
> If I had not been able to pay my own expenses, I could not possibly have lived with Mama because she was one very bossy lady. She had fixed opinions about everything. Without my own paycheck, I could not have entertained my friends, bought the clothes and furniture I liked, gone on the vacations I dreamed of, or cooked the food I preferred. For Mama, had she had control over my income, would have dictated all of that to me. I'm sure of that because she tried to do so everyday of my life for sixty-three years. But thanks to my job, I was able to say to her, when she became the household authority on something: "We don't agree with each other on this. So you do it your way, and I'll do it my way." [January 1983]

Paid work also constituted an opportunity for these single women to contribute to a world larger than their private world. Much like the never-married women of Britain's middle classes in the mid-nineteenth century, whom Martha Vicinus studied, the single women of this study "believed passionately in the morally redeeming power of work."[13]

Repeatedly, the women discussed their employment in terms of its moral worth to themselves and its social worth to their environment. The comments of a former social worker are representative:

> From the time I can remember, I wanted to figure out a way to make a difference. I didn't have particularly grand conceptions of what that might mean, but I did feel that I owed something to the world. Maybe it was a bit of *noblesse oblige* thinking that came my way because of the central place my father and mother held in the world of Skarmy, the small town I grew up in. Maybe it was survivor's guilt, since my identical twin died in infancy. But whatever the explanation, I knew that I had to find a way to make a contribution if I was going to keep my self-respect intact. Work with foster children gave me that opportunity. [February 1984]

The women who were employed in social work, teaching, nursing, medicine, and libraries spoke frequently (and easily) about the sense of mission that they attached to their work. Yet the never-married women in working-class occupations, with less obvious and less fully elaborated humanitarian rationales, also initiated discussion of the social and moral value of their paid work—in households, offices, factories, and retail stores. A former domestic worker described the place that her work held in her moral universe and in that of her employers:

> Washing floors, doing laundry, vacuuming, ironing— that is hard, dirty stuff. No glory there. But that scrubbing and bending kept me whole, kept me close to

Jesus, kept me useful. The pay was pitiful, let me tell you. But I was able to keep my mind on the important things while I did those chores.

And I did something else, too, all those years I was a housemaid. In every cleaning job I kept over the years, there was a child or two or three at the house. I knew I had a talent for reaching children with my example. Even white, rich children. They saw how much I respected myself for doing a good job. They saw what hard work looked like. We had a lot of talks, my bosses' kids and me, about work, about self-respect, about respecting other people, no matter what their station in life. I might have been no more than a maid, but I was a proud one and a fine one. I made a mark on the character of those children, that you can be sure of. I never got to be a teacher in a classroom, but I did manage to teach in the kitchen and in the nursery. [June 1983]

Another never-married woman, who had worked as a secretary for many years, also talked about her contributions:

Maybe nobody else understood my worth at work but me. It would have been nice if they had, but it wasn't necessary. Because my work stood all by itself, with or without the praise of others. I put thought into my job, real caring. The other secretaries didn't usually understand why I took pride in a job that got so little money and respect. But the crucial thing to remember was that *I* was the judge of my work, nobody else. If I typed a document well, organized an event that went off smoothly, resolved a dispute in the office, I got pleasure.

I would look in the mirror and see a blue-ribbon worker. [July 1984]

The 20 women in the group of 50 who held professional or managerial jobs said they valued the work itself and the discretion they had (however limited) in determining the pace, direction, and content of their assignments. A former social worker discussed some of the choices she had made at work:

> Before I went to social work school, I was a secretary for twelve years. But I didn't like having somebody else make all the key decisions. So I decided to get some professional training. My first social work job after graduate school was at the Bureau of Vocational Rehabilitation.
>
> One of the reasons I stayed there for so long [thirty-three years] was that I had quite a bit of say, after a while, over which cases would be mine. I was most enthused about working with paraplegics, the people in the most desperate need of encouragement, skills development, and job finding. Unfortunately, there were many people who came through with such difficulties, mostly men injured in battle or in motorcycle accidents. In that job, I not only chose who I worked with, but I set my own priorities among my cases and with each client. [February 1984]

Twelve of the 17 professional women (the 4 schoolteachers, the pediatrician, the 3 nurses, one of the librarians, and 3 of the social workers) identified their work with children and youth as the aspect of their employment from which they derived the most meaning. Indeed, 9 of these 12 women said they had chosen their professions and jobs for the express purpose of tending to the needs of children and teenagers. The remarks of one of the nurses represent the thinking of these 12 professionals:

> My father lobbied hard to get me to work in his business with him. But selling hardware was simply not interesting to me. I had done that since I was a little kid on the weekends and in the summers.
>
> No—instead I was eager to try my hand at helping children who allowed nobody close to them. In college, I had studied psychology. I really wanted to become a child psychiatrist, but women did not go to medical school very often in 1919, the year I got my B.A.
>
> So, I went to nursing school, instead, and worked my way into psychiatric nursing. Autistic kids were my specialty. Sometimes I even succeeded in getting some of those children to reach across the great chasm between us and speak to me. [July 1984]

Paid work, then, provided these single women an enhanced sense of their social utility and moral efficacy. Through employment, moreover, these women established their only primary or *achieved* role in life, that of *worker*. Having opted out of the two "stations," those of wife and mother, that confer on most women their central place, status, and meaning in our society, these never-married women leaned heavily on their work role for identity and prestige. Paid work constituted the sole claim of never-married women for public recognition of their agency, responsibility, and social legitimacy.

The importance of paid work to never-married women makes them vulnerable to what Lewis Coser calls "greedy institutions," and workplaces are an important example. Greedy institutions "seek exclusive and undivided loyalty and they attempt to reduce the claims of competing roles and status positions on those they wish to encompass within their boundaries. Their demands on the person are omnivorous." They "are not typically marked by external coercion. Instead they tend to rely on voluntary compliance and evolve means of activating loyalty and commitment."[14]

As single people with no "counterclaims" of spouse or children, never-married women have more difficulty than married employees in establishing the legitimacy of their commitments to people and their responsibilities outside the workday, workweek, and workplace.[15] As women, most have been socialized to comply with the directives and requests of authorities, especially male authorities. These women workers also remained aware of their limited options if refusal to comply resulted in discharge. As breadwinners, never-married women understood the imperative of keeping a job that fed them, and in many cases their aging parents as well. The "greediest" demand on the never-married women I interviewed was imposed on all the 4 schoolteachers in my sample: the requirement that they remain single. Moreover, the work of labor economist V. K. Oppenheimer suggests that the experience of these teachers was characteristic. Oppenheimer found that, before 1929, the majority of public school systems in America would not hire married women as teachers. Roughly half the school systems required teachers to resign if they got married, and by 1930 the statistics had worsened. Only 23 percent of U.S. school systems would hire married women as teachers; 61 percent of the school systems required that married women resign. By 1941, only 13 percent of the school systems in the United States would hire married women. According to Oppenheimer, these strictures did not begin to loosen until the 1950s.[16]

School systems were not alone in this form of greed. Between 1910 and 1940, Kessler-Harris notes, some states and municipalities fired librarians and social workers, as well as teachers, if they married.[17] In a 1939 survey by the National Industrial Conference Board, historian Susan Ware found that of the 84 percent of the U.S. insurance companies that returned questionnaires, 65 percent of the banks and 63 percent of the public utilities fired or placed significant restrictions on women employees who married.[18]

A former librarian, who had worked as a single woman in a public library, had distinct views on the marital restrictions she had encountered:

> I never met anyone I wanted to marry. And yet, it infuri-
> ated me anew each year in January when the city re-
> quired all the females on the staff of the library to sign a
> declaration that we had not married in the previous
> twelve months. Some of the women on staff wrote on
> the form that they had gotten married during the year.
> They were in each case canned, no matter how long
> their length of service to the city and the library. Others
> lied on the declaration. Two women I worked with got
> caught in their lies and were promptly fired. None of
> the men of the staff, mind you, were ever asked to de-
> clare their marital status in an annual check.
>
> After the firing of the first woman, I organized a
> petition campaign among librarians and citizens to get
> her reinstated and to get rid of the regulation that re-
> quired us to remain single. We garnered 3,100 signa-
> tures and took them to City Council. The Council
> members, all married men, laughed us out of Council
> Chambers. They wouldn't even hear our arguments.
> [March 1982]

Employers were greedy in other ways as well. Many of the women reported they were asked to work overtime, to put in evening and weekend duty, and to make out-of-town trips on short notice. Several commented on their bosses' assumption that they had no lives outside of work that might interfere with their honoring sudden demands on their evening and weekend hours. A former administrative assistant expressed her resentment:

> The top salary I earned was $5,200 a year in 1962. For that grand sum, my boss asked the sun and the moon of me. Now I was always a committed and diligent secretary. I loved to work. But I did *not* appreciate 10 P.M. calls to come over to the office to take some dictation. Nor did I like 6 A.M. demands to be in the office by 7:00. Nor did I think it right that my boss accepted assignments without consulting me, which required me to cancel suddenly all social plans for days on end. I said "no" lots of times to my boss. But you can only say "no" so many times before your loyalty comes into question. [July 1984]

Many of the women suggested that it was not enough, in their bosses' eyes, that they did their jobs in a competent manner. Instead, women at various occupational levels said they were called on to demonstrate *devotion* as well as competence. Women's studies scholar Paula Hooper Mayhew suggests that never-married women were expected to view work as a "vocation" rather than as a job.[19] In light of her husbandless and childless state, a never-married woman was presumed to derive her reason for being from her work. A former nurse reflected on such expectations:

> My work was of great importance to me. I was one of the finest O.R. [operating room] nurses in the county. But pride in work is different from absorption in it. Lots of people, including the head of the O.R., thought that

nothing else mattered to me. He expected me to live, breathe, and die surgical nursing.

When I asked for vacation time, he denied it, saying that he needed me too much. Seven years went by before I finally realized that I should just take time off, whether or not he approved. [March 1983]

The never-married women who worked for employers and institutions that sought their "exclusive and undivided loyalty" responded in many ways. Some were wholly compliant; they not only honored their employers' demands, but internalized their bosses' constructions of reality. Others behaved in a compliant manner, although they resented the notion that they should subordinate their lives to work. Still others alternated between obedience and refusal to comply. A few resisted all (or most) attempts to monopolize their energy, time, and devotion. A former stenographer remembers:

The first six months on my job I established tl e rules about what I would and would not do. My predecessor had believed in doing anything and everything asked of her. Would she give up Christmas Day to get out an urgent proposal? You bet. Would she cancel her vacation plans to prepare a last-minute budget? But, of course. Would she stay late at the office, night after night, typing the annual report? Indeed.

Mr. Jackson wanted all those things from me, too. But I just kept refusing. He could have fired or demoted me at any time. He did not do that. Instead he kept me on through my many refusals. I guess he respected the work I did agree to do during the regular workweek. He and I worked together for twenty-nine years. He was

still trying to get me to bend on these matters in the last
years of my employment there. I never gave up my position on keeping to the forty-hour week. And he never
gave up his view that the job to be done came before all
other things.   [November 1983]

The Great Depression, approximately between the years 1929
and 1939 in the United States, had a dramatic short- and long-term
impact on the worklives of these never-married women. For the
women I interviewed who entered the Depression years as workers
already established in jobs, careers, and professional schools (82
percent), as well as the younger women I spoke with who were still
in school or college in 1929 (18 percent), similar occupational
consequences emerged from the economic hardship, scarcity, and
despair that gripped the nation during the 1930s. Three primary
effects of the Depression were evident in the worklives of these
women: (1) their economic centrality and responsibility to their
families increased as times got more and more difficult; (2) the
limitations on the choices of work open to women were exac-
erbated after 1929 by the notion that, in times of high unemployment, women should not hold jobs that men could do;
and (3) throughout the 1930s, and in many cases long after,
they retained those jobs that they had found or held during the
early part of the Depression.

The women whom I interviewed managed to find work and stay
employed throughout the Depression years, and as a result, they
became crucial breadwinners for their families. Their success in
staying employed supports the findings of students of Depression-
era labor history. For example, Kessler-Harris finds that women
were least represented in U.S. industries that were most damaged
by the Depression, and most represented in industries with the least
shrinkage.[20] Ruth Milkman explains this phenomenon by suggest-

ing that, in the 1930s, women worked primarily in sex-segregated occupations, such as clerical and service work. These jobs, or "support services" that were not sought by men, maintained the industries and institutions they were part of and proved crucial for organizational survival, even during production and personnel cutbacks. Milkman, in comparing men and women's unemployment rates during the Depression, found that men suffered markedly higher unemployment rates than women. Therefore, she concludes, the deterioration in major sectors of manufacturing had less effect on women's jobs (mostly service, clerical, and trade) than on men's. In short, women were somewhat insulated by the sex-typed labor market in many areas of production and sales.[21]

By staying in the paid labor force, even under such badly paid and sex-segregated conditions, these single women became economic mainstays when other family members lost their jobs, during an era when married women—their mothers, aunts, and sisters—encountered public hostility and, in some occupations, exclusionary regulations when they sought work.[22]

Of the 28 percent of the sample who supported their parents *completely* for five years or more, 16 percent did so for at least two years during the 1930s. Of the additional 62 percent who *partially* supported their parents over time, 40 percent did so for two years or more during the 1930s. One woman's memories of the 1930s recall the desperation of the Depression period and her family's total reliance on her bookkeeper's wages:

> When the market came crashing down, three of us were employed at the time—my father, my mother, and me. Dad was a Mox and Co. steamfitter, a well-paid man for 1929, who made seven times what I made keeping books. Mother was employed on the assembly line of the same shop Dad worked in. For awhile, it looked as

if we would make it through unscathed. Then the roof
fell in on us, in 1931. Mox's went bankrupt. Dad lost
his job, Mom lost hers, and my wages became the
whole loaf of bread. As if that were not trying enough,
my brother was laid off from his sales position the following year. He came back home to live with us and
didn't find steady work again until 1936, at which time
he moved back on his own.

Neither Mother nor Dad worked regular again until
the war. For twelve years, from 1931 until 1943, mine
was the only earnings we could absolutely count on at
home.

Everybody, including me, had sneered at my income
before the crash. Dad used to joke that my pay was only
good enough to get me to the altar in style. We all
stopped sneering when that measly wage became the
only floor under our feet. [July 1983]

Any dreams of escaping the ghetto of women's jobs into work
not traditionally done by women had to be deferred until the early
1940s. Opinion regarding women in the workplace during the Depression tolerated no "crossing over" into occupational ranks that
were commonly understood to be those of men. In a country
whose unemployment rate octupled between 1929 and 1933, the
first priority of government, and the public as well, was to get the
traditional breadwinners back to work.[23] Few people, in the government or public, noticed that bread was "won" by women as well
as men. Little, if any, sympathy was extended to women workers
who wanted to enter nontraditional job categories. In the 1930s,
such demands would have been deemed selfish and frivolous.

Hard times caused many American workers, among them never-
married women with breadwinning responsibilities, to hold fast to

the jobs they already had or had obtained at the start of the Depression. A passion for security, not "horizontal" or "vertical" mobility, characterized the workers and the unemployed of the 1930s. This conservatism in occupational ambition and reluctance to experiment befit a time of bread lines, apple sellers, and farm failures. A never-married woman, a former nurse, expressed the effects on her life of this all-consuming interest in security:

> My parents lost everything by 1933—their business, their savings, their house, their pride. They came to live with me since I still had a job at St. Margaret's Hospital. I clung to that job for dear life. I made no waves; I asked for no raises. One year, my supervisor urged me to ask for a promotion, especially since I had been "Employee of the Year" the year before. Not me. I was afraid of drawing attention to myself. . . .
>
> Other girls went off to the Army Corps during the war. I would have loved to have gone. Yet I felt responsible for Mom and Dad. I also was too scared to go. Not scared of the Corps, but of the thought that I might not be able to get my job back after the war. [September 1983]

Though the effects of the Depression on the economic and occupational status of these single women were similar across generational lines, some of the younger women emphasized that their ambitions had been nipped in the bud while they were still in grade school, high school, or college. Early in life, they developed what several women called a "Depression mentality," a proclivity for viewing life as a zone of possible or probable disaster, in which one must cling to the job or life situation that maximizes predictability and continuity.[24]

Retrospectively, these single women expressed ambivalence toward changes in their work lives. All had felt compelled to "play it safe" during the 1930s, though most remembered dreaming of more rewarding work. Many women experienced World War II as an opportunity to explore new jobs, skills, and continents, but nonetheless worried, throughout the 1941–1945 years, about retaining job security after the war. Few of the women were wholehearted, at any age, in either acceptance or rejection of occupational experimentation.

Was World War II a four-year anomaly in the worklives of never-married women, or the beginning of enduring transformation in their work possibilities? For women workers in the United States, Kessler-Harris argues, the war had few lasting effects: "The evidence offers little support to those who suggest that the war was either a turning point or a milestone. Neither the lives of women nor the way industry responded to them in the immediate postwar years suggest such a conclusion."[25] However, a more complicated argument emerges from the lives of never-married women workers. World War II introduced challenges and opportunities that permanently expanded the vocational options of never-married women who were *already* college-educated or professionally trained at the outbreak of the war. For women in the sample who did *not* have a B.A. or specialized skills in 1941, the war provided three to four years of occupational opportunity and substantially higher wages. For working-class women workers in 1945, demilitarization and "normalization" meant return to the clerical, factory, and service ranks that had paid them so little before 1941.

Sixteen of the 20 professional and managerial women whom I interviewed identified 1941–1945 as a seedtime for their subsequent careers. New vocational and training possibilities and unforeseen responsibilities and job contacts surfaced for them during this period. Of the 16 women who said they gained lasting advances from wartime, 10 spent these years in the Women's Army Corps (WAC) and 6 in professional or managerial positions outside the military. Both groups of professional women remembered the virtual explosion of opportunity they had faced in 1942 either as WACs or private citizens. A former nurse and former WAC reminisced:

> On Pearl Harbor Day [December 7, 1941], I was one of forty-odd nurses in a Catholic hospital in Philadelphia. Six months later, I was in charge of 145 nurses, paramedics, and orderlies in Simmons Army Hospital in Georgia. Still another six months later, I headed up all nursing services on a battleship in the South Pacific.
>
> They were heady times. I had no idea then that my life would be remade by the war. When I came back to the States, I was in great demand to help create rehabilitation units, to devise burn units, and to train psychiatric nurses. Hospitals and universities from all over the country wanted this Polish girl from St. John's Parish to come work for them as Director of Nursing. It's odd to make hay during a national catastrophe, but that is exactly what happened to me.   [December 1983]

A former teacher-turned-insurance executive described the war's "contributions" to her career:

> In my town, a woman never held an official position of leadership before 1942. Within the same month, I became Acting Principal of the high school and head of the local Red Cross. Both of those responsibilities kept me in the public eye and taught me about managing complex operations.

The press I got for running the county Red Cross office caught the attention of a vice-president of the Wichita Insurance Company. Throughout the war, he would periodically drop me a note that read: "Keep Wichita Insurance Company in mind whenever you get tired of teaching." In 1948, I got tired of teaching. Sure enough, Joe Simms remembered me and made me an offer I couldn't refuse.   [April 1982]

Although these postwar advancements and changes in career were foreign to the experience of the working-class women with whom I spoke, they remembered the dramatic (though ephemeral) upheavals caused by World War II between 1942 and 1945. Many took production jobs in heavy manufacturing that, in peacetime, were closed to women. Seventeen of the 30 women who held jobs that in 1941 were other than professional or managerial, shifted from clerical, service, or sales jobs to factory work during the war. Their pay increased significantly while they learned particularized skills, such as welding, steam fitting, and electrical and electronic wiring. One woman, who had been a secretary in 1941, then found a job that trained her to repair auto and Jeep engines, commented:

For almost three years, I made an excellent living. Working on cars earned me more than three times what typing had. I dearly loved that work and the things it taught me. But I knew that it wouldn't last. I never thought otherwise. Why would a country that had kept women out of good-paying jobs since the Pilgrims landed suddenly change all that? Who would type their

letters after the war for a pittance if women were permitted to be auto mechanics?   [July 1984]

Working-class black women, in particular, made rapid employment shifts soon after the start of the war. Leaving domestic work
and cooking behind at the first opportunity, 5 of these women took
jobs in heavy industry that lasted until the war's end. One woman's
reflections (below) support the claim of Jacqueline Jones[26] that
black women workers viewed wartime as a "Utopia" of high wages
and employment possibilities:

> Can you imagine what it is like to suddenly have doors
> open that had been nailed shut since I was born? The
> word went out in my neighborhood that the local
> factories were desperate for workers—even black
> workers—even black females. I had been cleaning
> houses, like most girls I knew, when I learned the news.
> I rushed out to apply for work, not really believing
> that it would be available. But sure enough, Coscomb's
> took me right away because all their production line-
> men had enlisted. They paid me at rates I never
> dreamed that I would ever earn. It all came to a screech-
> ing halt, of course, at the end of the war. I went back to
> domestic work in 1947, after eighteen months of
> knocking on the doors of places that suddenly had no
> use for my production skills.   [December 1982]

During the war, some working-class single women (13 of the 30
I interviewed) stayed within the occupations they had been part of
before December 1941. Most of these 13 said they had been given
expanded authority and responsibilities in their workplaces when
key men went off to the war. Some changed jobs, within their

occupation, to earn more pay and gain more autonomy. One woman, a former bookkeeper, spoke about the larger responsibility she found during wartime:

> At Stokes', I had loads of responsibility but little authority. The chief accountant took all the credit for my bookkeeping acumen. He was too old to go to the Army, so nothing much changed for me at Stokes' when the war broke out.
>
> When I read in the *Herald* of a head bookkeeping job available at the largest corporation in this area, I decided to try for it. Sure enough, I got it and quadrupled my salary overnight. Suddenly, I had twenty-eight girls working for me. I was in heaven at that job, even though I knew it was the nightmare of the war that put me in that heaven. [April 1983]

For a combination of material and symbolic reasons, paid work became a linchpin of these women's lives. In the decades after the war, however, they had to adjust to the consequences of leaving their work behind, as retirement, illness, and age became new factors to deal with. In leaving behind paid work, the women lost much more than their pay; they left the arena that had assured them dignity, status, and camaraderie. After retiring, they therefore turned to long-standing sources of meaning and friendship and to new alternatives.

SIX / Aging and Retirement: A Study in Continuity

I have never understood all the to-do made over old age. I'm the same person who I have always been, except now my joints speak to me on bad days. And now I have no schedule that anyone else imposes on me.

Last month I turned eighty-nine. Youngsters round me "oohed and ahed" and talked to me in that condescending way people have when they have reduced you in their minds to the status of living decrepit wonder. But I am no living wonder. And I'm certainly not decrepit. I'm just somebody who pursues the same things in life that I did at twenty: good companionship, good food, and good works.   [August 1983]

After retirement, the lives of these 50 never-married women closely resemble their lives before retirement. Indeed, many saw their retirement as a chance to capitalize on the "free time" never before available to them as adults. This meant furthering relationships and activities they had long enjoyed, but in forms more self-determined and idiosyncratic than they had known during full-time employment.

Twenty-three of the never-married women voluntarily retired; that is, they said they had ended their full-time jobs when they wanted to retire. More than half of the women (27) retired involuntarily; that is, they left full-time employment before they wanted to, because of their own illness; or because of care-giving responsibilities for sick, disabled, or dying family members; or because laws or regulations forced them to retire.

One of every 5 women I interviewed, 10 in all, retired early and voluntarily, either to end the frustration and exhaustion they had experienced on the job or to pursue more compelling interests. All 4 public schoolteachers retired early by choice, in their late fifties or early sixties, because they were dissatisfied with their working conditions. One of the schoolteachers said:

> Things went from good to bad to worse in the 1960s. Faculty morale slipped badly when the principals stopped backing up our authority, when young teachers came in who cared more about contract terms than about children, when students grew more and more unruly, and when parents increasingly interfered with classroom matters. A great shift in attitudes took place in my district right about 1966 or 1967. Respect for teaching took a nosedive while litigiousness among

students, parents, and teachers soared. Student rights, parent rights, union power, and community control displaced the learning process as central concerns. [December 1982]

Others chose to retire early in order to develop second careers or to explore activities, relationships, or places that had appealed to them for years. The comments of one of these women are representative:

For thirty-six years I deeply enjoyed my job as a caseworker and psychotherapist in a strict Freudian agency. Early retirement posed the possibility of retraining as a structural family therapist. I could not have done that sort of treatment and kept my senior position at the Simpkin Youth and Children Center. There the doctrinal requirements were quite clear. Just mention Gestalt psychology, Jungian theory, or family therapy in an approving manner, and you are looking for a new job.

So I retired at fifty-nine and went to study in an institute that conceptualized relationships and change in a wholly different way than that which I had known before. It has been a grand experiment. I cherish both careers—the one before I retired and the private practice I have developed in family therapy since age fifty-nine. [July 1984]

Part-time work was important during their old age to 22 of the 50 women. Most of the 22 had worked in part-time jobs that were similar to the jobs they had performed earlier on a full-time basis. A few women, like the nurse-turned-horticulturalist (below), started a new career after retiring. The motivation for working part-time during retirement was usually complicated, as in the case of the retired nurse who responded:

> Why have I kept working in retirement? Money, dear, I need money. Social security is peanuts, and so are my savings. But I also work to stay in touch with people I would not otherwise meet. After forty-odd years as an emergency room nurse, I can't just throw away all that delicious diversity. How else would I encounter teenagers and people of every race and persuasion?
>
> Besides which, I like to stay useful. I only work twelve hours a week now, but that is enough to make a bit of a difference in a few patients' lives.
>
> And I should also say that I keep working to keep from spending my days thinking about my aches and pains. Like most oldsters, I have my share. If I didn't work, I would make my joint creaks a full-time preoccupation.   [April 1983]

More than half the women retired involuntarily (27) and those who were most distressed by retirement were the 9 women who were compelled to stop by retirement laws or company regulations. They were outraged at the arbitrariness of age limitations:

> The worst part of it is the dishonesty involved. My bosses kept talking about "my golden years" and my "well-deserved rest." What they weren't saying is what they really thought—that they wanted to make room for younger people whom they could pay less and hoodwink more.
>
> One day I'm the brains behind the operation. The next day I am expendable because my birthday came

and went. The fact is that I was a fine contributor when I was made to retire at seventy. I worked a full eight-hour day and stayed up with new trends and technology as well as any of them. They threw me on the scrap heap because of a company rule that failed to take into account the enormous variation in capacity of people who are old. It is obvious to me that the company lost as much as I did in the process.   [June 1982]

In order to care for aging or sick family members, 10 other women (20 percent of the total) terminated full-time work that they would have liked to continue. In the absence of publicly provided or subsidized in-home care for the aged, chronically ill, and disabled, these women faced the dilemma of choosing between work and family commitments, and most of them chose to assist their parents or siblings. On the whole, they did not reject care-giving, but the presumption that women—in particular single women—should bear the full weight of long-term geriatric care. One woman stated her position with special force:

If I saw any men in our family retiring to care for their mothers, I might not mind so much the early retirement that I was obligated to take. Not one voice was raised to question: "But what about Nancy's life? What would this do to her?"

Instead, my brothers and sisters ducked the whole debate about how our family should proceed in a society that doesn't give a damn about ailing old people. They hid behind marriage and children. I had no official bodies to hide behind. Meanwhile, Mother was in dreadful shape, and we could not pay for a decent nursing home. I was not being a martyr. There were simply no other choices which I could have stomached.

The job I gave up was a pearl. It took me twenty-one years to work up to that position of authority. Four years later I gave it up when Mother's diabetes cost her her leg.   [May 1982]

Another group of forced retirees was the 8 women whose illnesses or disabilities put an end to their full-time employability. It goes without saying, perhaps, that they were the most resigned to their lot of all the women who retired involuntarily. Though they would have preferred to continue working full-time, they had retired because of pain, exhaustion, or debilitation. Their firsthand experience with illness forced them to acknowledge the limitations imposed by acute or chronic disease or disability. One woman, whose vision failed in her late fifties, reflected on her retirement at sixty-three:

How can a librarian work without her vision? I was head of acquisitions and needed to keep up in a daily way with new books and periodicals coming out. A librarian without eyesight is like a surgeon without fingers.

With the deepest sadness, I resigned early. I had hoped to work to seventy, at the very least. Yet that was not to be in the great scheme of things. It took me a couple of years to come to terms with my retirement and my bad vision.   [September 1983]

The act of ending full-time employment connoted, for some of the women, a sense of loss—loss of identity as a worker and a colleague, loss of a daily schedule, of social contacts, of productivity, and of income. To others, retirement meant freedom from obligations, bureaucracies, bosses, and workaday regimens. To still others, retirement meant the opportunity to renew old commitments or experiment with new ones. Most of the women attributed two or three of these meanings to their retirement—for example:

> What a conglomeration of things I feel and felt about retiring. I was alternately overjoyed, downcast, and uncertain. One day I felt like a lost shoe, the next like a woman with worlds to conquer. The very best part is not having a strict schedule anymore. If I want to sleep till noon, I do so. If I want to walk at dawn, I do that too.
>
> It is quite a complicated business to live a full life as a retired person in a world whose axis is the workday. It requires that I find a central axis of my own that will orient me without the help of anyone else. [June 1984]

Old age demands not only that never-married women find their "central axis" and orient themselves, but also that they pay their way economically. Thus, despite retirement, their lives are continuations of patterns established throughout adulthood.

What are the economic realities of single women in old age? The never-married women I interviewed fared slightly worse in income than women in general who were sixty-five and older in 1983 (except at the extreme bottom of the income groupings). Of the women I interviewed, 58.1 percent had an annual income of under $6,000, compared with 55.3 percent of all women in the United States and 25.7 percent of all men. In other words, one of every 2 women I interviewed lived on less than $6,000 a year in 1983, when $11,718 was the median income in the United States for people sixty-five years old and over.[1] Viewed another way, 44.2 percent (19 of 43) of the women I interviewed lived below the poverty level in 1983, a year in which 15.2 percent of all Americans lived below the poverty level.[2] (Officially, the poverty level for an individual sixty-five years old or older, living alone, was $4,775 in 1983. For someone sixty-five or older who lived in a two-person household, the poverty level was $6,023.)[3]

Social security payments were the most important source of income, by far, for these never-married women, even though 11 of the 43 had worked in jobs not covered by social security laws. Social security was the *only* source of income for 19 of the women. Private or governmental pensions supplemented social security for only 18 of the 43 women. Those 25 women who did not receive a private or governmental pension had either worked for employers who did not offer pensions or they had retired before the terms of the Employee Retirement Income Security Act of 1974 came into effect. (This act protects now-retired workers who do not receive pensions because their employers' pension plans were terminated, or employers went bankrupt, or the companies or factories closed before the workers reached retirement age.)[4]

Public assistance, most commonly Supplemental Security Income (S.S.I.), was the sole source of income for 3 of the women and a partial source for 8 others. Earnings during retirement were an important source of income for 22 of the 43 women, as were savings (for 30 of the 43 women). The percentage of these single women who worked after retirement, 51 percent, far outstrips the labor-force rate of 7.8 percent for all women aged sixty-five and older in 1983.[5] Apparently, these never-married women participated in the labor force, after age sixty-five, at a rate almost seven times the national average, because their need for money converged with their long-held commitments to work.

From a variety of sources—part-time work, social security, pensions, public assistance, and savings, which many of the women somehow compiled while working—these women managed to survive. Retirement and old age, however, raise questions of independence and dependence that they have faced throughout their lives. As one of these women said:

> I am the first to bristle when married people or youngsters bandy about old ideas about "old maids." I set them straight right away about what single women are like. Mostly I make sure that they comprehend that ten single women present at least ten different approaches to living.
>
> But I also know that we single women *do* share some qualities in common out of necessity. For example, we tend to plan ahead; we're good savers; and we initiate lots of things. Emily Post, you see, never devised a trail guide for the single woman. One has to devise that trail guide for herself at each step. So we do. From the outside, that looks like we are independent in the extreme. From the inside, I would say instead that we are heavily dependent on ourselves as well as on those select ones we choose to lean on.   [April 1983]

Another strategy these women employed to maintain economic continuity in old age was to share a household and pool expenses and resources with a friend or family member. For 22 of the 50 women, sharing a household in retirement meant continuing a long-established tradition. But for 24 of the 50, moving into a joint living arrangement was something new in old age. These 24 women preserved economic continuity by sacrificing domestic continuity.

> When I reached age fifty, I took a hard look at my savings and at my income and at my projected piddling

pension. I imagined myself at age seventy, scrounging around for bus fare, just to get to church on Sunday morning.

It occurred to me then that living on my own works swell when I am healthy and bringing in a living wage. But what would happen to me if my oh-so-independent body decided to become old, all of a sudden? And how would I manage on the few dollars I figured would be mine in retirement?

Everything pointed me towards making a change. I decided that I should convince a friend to share an apartment with me after we retired. We could share the costs of a household and be good company for each other, when there no longer would be the work companions nearby that I so obviously relied on. Happily, my best friend thought that mine was a first-rate idea. She liked the proposal so much, in fact, that we began living together when I was fifty-five, rather than at sixty-five. (She was a year younger than me.) I'm now eighty-seven, Martha is eighty-six, and we've lived together swimmingly these thirty-two years. We're certainly *not* in the money, you understand, but we do get through by joining forces and bankbooks. [December 1982]

The foresighted adaptiveness of this woman was common among these never-married women, but she was the only one who moved in with a friend in or near retirement. The other 23 women who created joint living arrangements in old age did so with family members. Twenty-two other women remained in retirement in joint households that they had created as young or middle-aged adults, and 14 of them were in "Boston marriages" (long-term, "passionate" friendships between two women who shared a home over time). Eight women continued to live with a sibling. Only 4 of the women lived alone at the time of their interviews.

This pattern deviates sharply from the national pattern. As Table 9 indicates, 40.9 percent of all women in the United States, sixty-five and over, lived alone in 1983—five times the rate for the women I interviewed. The well-documented tendency of women to live longer than men is part of the explanation, and married women usually live as part of a couple, in retirement with their husbands (although by age seventy-five, two-thirds of these women are widowed).[6] By contrast, the never-married women I interviewed lived with other women in 42 of the 46 cases (4 women lived with a brother). Moreover, these women may go through life with an awareness of several choices for a household companion, rather than a single possibility, a husband.

Unlike married women, never-married women generally approach late middle age and old age as people solely in charge of their economic fate. Thus never-married women have formed the

TABLE 9 / Living Arrangements of Women 65 and Older (by Race and Hispanic Origin, 1983)

Living Arrangement	Percentage			
	All Races	White	Black	Hispanic
With husband	38.7	39.7	27.0	29.1
With family members or nonrelatives	20.4	18.7	36.1	39.3
Alone	40.9	41.7	36.8	31.9

Source: Computed from Bureau of the Census, Current Population Reports, Series P-20, No. 389 (Washington, D.C.: U.S. Government Printing Office, 1984), Table 6.

habit of planning ahead with great care, and for the large majority of these women, their planning involved keeping or finding a roommate with whom to live after retirement.

Finally, never-married women have far less household income throughout adulthood, and especially during ages fifty-five to sixty-four, than do married couples. As a consequence, single women who are thinking about retirement learn firsthand about the limits of single women's income long before most women in intact marriages encounter such limitations in widowhood. Never-married women, approaching retirement age, have already derived, from their direct experience with low wages and salaries (their only source of income), the conclusion that retirement would be more livable with two incomes than with one. They therefore search their families and friendship networks for someone who can offer both compatibility and solvency. At the time of the interviews, the 50 never-married women whom I studied lived in the kinds of arrangements shown in Table 10. All 19 of the women who lived

TABLE 10 / Living Arrangements of 50
Never-Married Retired Women

Living Arrangement	Alone	With Friend(s)	With Family Members
Boarding house	1		
Rental apartment	1	5	12
Own home, condominium, or cooperative	1	4	11
Own apartment within retirement home or community	1	5	8
Own house within retirement community		1	

alone or with a friend said they were satisfied with their arrangements. Those few women who lived alone emphasized the importance to them of the independence that living by themselves provided. For example:

> Certainly, I take obvious risks living by myself at this age [eighty-three]. I could fall and break my hip without anybody knowing. I could get mugged coming home from a meeting or from shopping.
>
> Those risks are quite clear to me, but even clearer are the gains I reap from solo living. The biggest gain is that I get to keep my own ways. Nobody tells me how to be. My friends come visit often, so I have ample fun. But I don't have to rearrange my life for anybody. I don't have to accommodate anyone else's ups and downs. That is just how I want things until death do me part.   [May 1984]

The 15 women who lived with friends were similarly pleased with their lot. Fourteen of them had lived with the same woman friend for several decades before retirement, and only one woman began living with a friend after retiring. These 15 women, not surprisingly, emphasized different priorities than did the 4 who lived alone. One woman who lived with a friend said:

> I long ago chose companionship over privacy. Elizabeth and I worked out a mutually acceptable *modus vivendi* in our first years as housemates, back in 1938. This arrangement is far and away the best for me. We are the best of friends and therefore know when and how to let the other be. She takes care of me, and I of her. We are completely dependent on each other and utterly inde-

pendent at the same time. That may sound contradictory, but it is not. We lean on each other immeasurably, but carve out, each of us, our own path. When one of us dies, the other will carry on somehow. Sadly, painfully, gropingly, God knows, but nonetheless assuredly. [July 1983]

Mixed reviews on their household situations emerged from the 31 women who lived with a member or members of their family. Most (26) lived with a sister; 4 lived with a brother; one lived with a niece. Of these 31, 10 expressed unreserved praise for their shared households; 13 spoke with ambivalence about the wisdom of their choice; and 8 regretted their decision to live with a sibling. The dissatisfactions expressed by the following woman locate her among the ambivalent:

Fear of poverty in my last years led me to ask Kate [a younger sister] to live with me. I thought I had weighed carefully all the pros and cons. Most of them I foresaw. For example, I knew we would help each other financially, and I knew that she is a person of unquestionable integrity. However, what I forgot to calculate was the cumulative effect of living with someone who whines instead of talking. When we were kids, I could not stand Kate's whining. But back then Momma usually made her stop. Nowadays, there is no Momma to get her back on track. I try my best, but usually she just whines more when I object to her complaining tone of voice. I am a good Christian, so I try to live and let live. Some days, though, I just want to put her possessions out on the street and change the locks. Only a louse would actually do that, but what a fine fantasy it is. [January 1984]

Some women expressed disappointment:

> How could I have so underestimated the difficulties of
> living with Rubie [a sister]? We had lived together grow-
> ing up. I thought I had a complete picture of what I was
> getting into.
>
> But she has changed since childhood. She has forgot-
> ten how to laugh. She mourns for her husband most of
> the time, though he is dead now twelve years. It is as if
> she lost her capacity to embrace life when Charlie [her
> husband] died. I truly thought her black mood would go
> away with time. But it doesn't. If I could do it financially,
> I would go my own way. But that is out of the question
> completely now. I sunk everything I have into the down
> payment on this place. The only thing I can do now is
> compensate by seeing my friends at every opportunity
> and making the best of things.   [March 1983]

The 16 women who lived in their own houses, condominiums,
or cooperative residences took pride in their ownership, regardless
of whether they enjoyed the relationships within them. Ten had
bought their house or apartment in middle age, after years of sav-
ing money; six had inherited their residences from their parents
and had lived all or most of their lives in them. Both sets of owners
articulated deep attachment to the places in which they lived. Only
one of these 16 women expressed doubts about her ability to stay
in her home for the rest of her days, whereas the other 15 indicated
a strong commitment to staying in their residence:

> Do you think I spent twenty years paying for this place
> only to wander off near the end like a stray dog? Susan
> [a sister] and I plan to remain here and keep our garden
> and play canasta with our neighbors until such time as

the Grim Reaper appears for each of us. We have talked about what it will be like when one of us goes. We have considered our options. Nothing could get us to move from here. If we get sick or stuck in wheelchairs, the visiting nurses will help us out, or we'll ask neighbors to fix us meals. We Samson sisters have always made it on our own before. I see no reason to believe that we cannot navigate old age as skillfully as we steered the rest of our course.   [June 1982]

The 15 women who lived in a retirement home or community communicated clear satisfaction with their living arrangements. Each had thought out her retirement plans long before the age of sixty-five, and most had saved for old age throughout their working years. All reported that they had chosen a retirement home or community to ensure that they would be taken care of in the event that ill health or senility made them dependent on others. The thoughtful pragmatism that informed their planning for old age also dominated their reflections on their life in a retirement setting. These comments are an example:

This is my tenth year here at St. John's. I get out of this place exactly what I expected—companionship, cultural stimulation, and the assurance that a skilled nurse or hospital is *always* available to me for the same fee that shelters and feeds me.

When I was in my forties, I broke a hip and was laid up for three months in my apartment. That calamity started me thinking about the last part of my life to come. There was no way I would be able to fend for myself at eighty, if my hip broke again. Sure, I had lived with a close friend since I was in high school. But I could not be sure Yolanda would live forever nor that she would be in good health when I might need her, nor vice versa. As it turned out, she got run over by a car a few years before I moved here. If I had planned my old age around Yolanda, I would have been in a sorry state, indeed. I miss her awfully, but I've got a rich life here, just as she would have wanted for us both. [November 1983]

In contrast to independent homeowners and residents of retirement institutions, the 18 women who lived in rental apartments, separate from retirement or life-care settings, showed no particular "investment" in the physical dimension of their living arrangements nor confidence in their capacity to control their length of stay there. The renters, as a group, expressed uncertainty—about their landlords' plans, about the likelihood of their neighborhoods' remaining livable for an old person, and about their future health and mobility.

Most members of this group of renters, 13 of 18, portrayed themselves as people in transition. Some were searching for a retirement home or community; some were trying to purchase a cooperative apartment; some were hoping that they could soon buy the apartment they were currently renting; and some were planning to move into the home of a friend or relative. One of these "renters in transition" discussed her hunt for a more secure living arrangement:

To be a renter in 1984 in Philadelphia is to be at the mercy of the greed of realtors and landlords. I live on a fixed income, but our landlord counts on an ever-expanding income. He increases the rent every year as much as the law permits, and I have, therefore, that much less to live on every time he does.

So it shouldn't surprise you that my sister and I look for a more stable situation. Like a life-care community. Those are places that give you an independent apartment and community meals, if you want them. Then, for the initial money down and a set monthly fee, they provide health care when you need it.

My sister and I have put our names on the waiting list of one of those places. If we get accepted, we will sell everything we have and own, and turn over all our possessions to the institution. In return, we will get a place of security and a ready-made community of people who are struggling with the same vicissitudes of old age in America that we are. [July 1984]

With few exceptions, the never-married women with whom I spoke viewed old age as a time in which to pool resources and share living quarters with a friend or sibling. For roughly half the women, sharing a household meant discontinuing a pattern of living alone, after several decades. For another large portion, 44 percent, a shared residence in retirement was merely a continuation of habits established in early or mid-adulthood. Living alone, in short, was a choice that few of these never-married women invoked in old age. As long-independent women, they—as a group— wanted to exercise control over the conditions in which they might have to endure physical or financial dependency in their future. Therefore, long ahead of time, they had chosen the people with whom and the places in which they would live out the last third of their lives.

Their desire to take charge of some dimensions of old age was accompanied, in many of the women, by a realistic sense of their inability to control the physical components of aging. The following woman's comments capture this realism:

> I figure I am doing terrifically for an eighty-two-year-old. My dentures fit. My eyes still read well enough to convince me that this country is in big trouble, and my arthritis slows me down, but it rarely, praise God, keeps me down. At eighty-two, who doesn't have such difficulties? I have no time for oldsters who moan about their failing bodies. When bodies get old, they don't work so well as when they're new. It is that simple. Life is far too short to worry about a little pain or some missing parts. Unless you are in major pain, just shut up and keep rowing. I have all the physical resources I need. After all, I am alive; my aches and pains usually know their place; and I am fully able to take my constitutional walk every day before dinner. If my body says, "Slow down," I slow down. If my mind says, "Take a nap," I take a nap. Getting old is not the big deal people sometimes claim it is. It is a simple exercise in figuring out your limits and going just an inch beyond them. [August 1984]

The same adaptiveness that informed these never-married women's approaches to consolidating housing and living arrangements in retirement characterized their attitudes toward the physiological changes of old age. On the whole, they said little about their health, unless I questioned them about their physical status. With only a few exceptions, illness and disability appeared to be secondary concerns of these never-married women. They had their share of health problems (as Table 11 notes), but considered them an inevitable part of old age.

TABLE 11 / Illnesses and Disabilities of 50 Never-Married Women

Illness or Disability	Number of Women
Arthritis or bursitis	32
Loss of vision	
Total	2
Major	4
Minor	13
Loss of hearing	
Total	1
Major	9
Minor	20
Heart condition	6
Hypertension	15
Diabetes	11
Confined to wheelchair	
Completely	3
Sometimes	7
Required walker	
Always	3
Sometimes	5
Parkinson's disease	3
Cancer	
At time of interview	2
In the past	6
Gastrointestinal disorders	7
Miscellaneous illnesses	7

The stoicism toward pain, sickness, and disability that these women (on the whole) demonstrated sprang not from denial but from resignation and familiarity with the physical difficulties that often accompany old age. Most of the women (42) had been the primary caretaker during a parent or sibling's chronic or terminal illness, and this exposure, before their own old age, to sickness, chronicity, and dying among their relatives left many of them sober realists about the predictability of health problems in old age. Care-giving, in short, seems to have prepared this group of women, early and well, to take their own physical deterioration in stride. These comments are similar to those expressed by many:

> Mom and Dad both went out the long and painful way. Mom was sick for nine months; Dad for eighteen months. I took careful note of the things old age did to them long before they got really sick. None of it seems a big deal to me, except the final, ghastly sickness. Cancer scares me because it killed them both. But they each stayed pretty healthy until that time. Eighty-two and seventy-six years of healthy living, respectively, is not bad.
>
> I am seventy-eight now, and have little to complain about. I lost a breast and a leg years ago. But I do fine without them. I have good energy, clear vision, and loads of friends. What more does a girl need, except a good read in the evening?   [May 1984]

As women without children to care for them in old age and as people familiar with the effects of aging in their seventh, eighth, and ninth decades of living, most of the retired women, regardless of social class, had taken steps to assure themselves of a setting and companion that could afford them comfort and care if sickness struck. Planning appears to have supplanted worrying in their preparations for retirement. However, their relaxed and philosophical response to health problems did not extend to paying for health care and medications. Health care costs were a frequent topic of complaint and source of worry. Even the women who were able to purchase Medicare and its special, attached coverage had difficulty paying bills that were not covered, or only partially covered, by their plans.

Community—at church; in volunteer, professional, or political organizations; in the neighborhood; or in a retirement institution—was of major importance to these women, who had built ties to groups of people outside their family and workplace long before they reached the age of sixty-five.

> Upon retiring, I had the chance at last to join wholeheartedly in my church's goings on in the way I had wanted to since I was a child. I'm not talking just Sunday mornings. I'm talking Thursday evening Bible study, Wednesday afternoon social action committee, Sunday afternoon visiting of shut-ins, and Monday evening meetings of the Board of Elders of the church. They call me a pillar of my church, but the reverse is closer to the truth. My church and its congregants anchor me, not vice versa.   [July 1982]

The 45 women in the group who had been active in their communities before they retired, then continued to be similarly active and committed after they retired. The 5 women who had chosen a more isolated life while working full-time, remained barely involved in organizational or neighborhood activity after they retired. These retired women's community commitments are manifest in the finding that each woman contributed, on average, 18.3 hours per week of volunteer work to the causes or organizations of her choice. The breadth and depth of the women's participation is detailed in Table 12.

This heavy or frequent participation in community groups served several purposes. It provided crucial social contacts, a formal social role, and an opportunity to contribute to the social good. For most of these women, church and community organizations had long been significant parts of their lives, and when their full-time paid work ceased, this volunteer work may have compensated them. At any rate, most of the religious and community groups that are central to these women are intergenerational, and a few, especially those in retirement villages or communities, have only retirees as members. For the most part, the women I interviewed belonged to both types of organizations at once—that is, to those that are intergenerational and those that are more or less homogeneous in age. They said that they worked in mixed-age groups in order to contribute to a diverse social whole and to keep

TABLE 12 / Frequency of Community Activities of
50 Never-Married Women

Volunteer or Group Activity	Daily	2–3 Times a Week	Weekly	Bi-weekly	Monthly
Church	7	15	21	3	1
Community service or charity	3	12	19	3	4
Cultural	2	10	9	4	5
Neighborhood or block	1	9	8	3	2
Senior citizen	2	7	20	7	8
Political	2	6	9	8	7
Professional		4	7	9	11

abreast of changing values and behavior. One woman described her involvement this way:

> I love my seniors' bunch that meets every week here. I wouldn't miss it even once, unless I was under the weather.
>
> But I also want to sustain regular contact with all ages of people. If I am going to "stay hip," I have got to listen to the rhythms of many generations. Kids talk to me, the teenagers come by, young mothers drop in, and middle-aged couples ask me to dinner. Why? Because I work hard at the YMCA and meet the entire spectrum of Philadelphians that way. That offers essential spice to my life.   [December 1983]

With only 3 exceptions, the women's participation in mixed-age organizations did not constitute denial of old age and dissociation from other old people, as sociologist Irving Rosow asserts.[7] Instead, the women consider themselves old people who are "stretching," through work with younger people, across the age continuum. Indeed, many spoke appreciatively of the rewards they derive from belonging to groups of old people, emphasizing many of the same benefits that Arlie Russell Hochschild observed in the public housing project for senior citizens in San Francisco. Like Hochschild's residents of Merrill Court, the women I interviewed said they gain mutual aid, friendship, role clarification, humor, and an antidote to loneliness in their senior citizens' groups.[8]

One woman's comments about concomitant membership in same-age and intergenerational organizations were representative:

> You just can't get everything from one source. I look to my old ladies' group for confirmation that "old is beau-

tiful." I also learn from them how to laugh at my rainy-day rheumatism and at the insults that youngsters sometimes hurl at old women.

But when I want to be pushed to reexamine my perceptions and beliefs about what's going on, I go to the Big Brother/Big Sister group I am on the board of. I take part each week in their program for pregnant teenagers and teenage mothers and learn a ton each time about the pressures that life brings these days to fifteen-year-olds. Then I do my best to bring fifteen-year-olds' thoughts to the eighty-five-year-olds in my senior women's group.   [June 1984]

The story of these 50 never-married women is primarily one of the continuity of predilections and relationships established earlier in adulthood. Nevertheless, a subplot of discontinuity breaks through from time to time: the loss of loved ones. Given the women's close relationships with family and friends, it is not surprising that old age brings a series of telling and disruptive losses. One woman generalized her experience in old age with the death of intimates:

Once you get past seventy-five, you have to somehow come to terms with the fact that most of the people you have shared your life with are dropping like flies. You have to squeeze the best out of every minute of an evening with a buddy 'cause he may be gone within the year. You have to seize every opportunity to show someone how deeply you care, as that may be your last chance to do so.

Do I sound grim? I do not mean to. I just put in stark terms a rather stark reality—that death becomes a potent force in your seventh decade of living that *must* be reckoned with each time it strikes. [January 1983]

At the time of the interviews, 22 of the 50 never-married women were mourning a friend or family member who had died within the previous twelve months. Another 18 women grieved for companions or relatives who had died within thirty-six months of the interviews. The statement of one woman speaks for the grief of many:

> My life was turned on its head when Molly died. She and I lived together for thirty-nine years, shared our friends, shared all our expenses, shopped together, and prayed together. That first year after she passed on was a living hell. Everything I did brought back memories of her. Gardening, marketing, entertaining, reading, traveling suddenly held no meaning for me without her. [August 1984]

This woman's experience, and that of most of the others, is dramatically different from the experience described by Jaber Gubrium in his study of single elders:

> Being single in old age is a kind of premium. Since such persons have no spouses, they do not experience the social disruptions that come with the death of the spouse. Their everyday routines are more likely than [the routines of] the married to have been generated out of lifelong relative isolation.[9]

The reflections of the women I interviewed diverge sharply from both of Gubrium's conclusions: that (1) people without spouses do not experience major social disruptions from death in old age, and

(2) single women live isolated lives. The first notion's implied claim of privileged status for spousal intimacy disregards the depth of intimate relationships that the never-married often develop; and the second conclusion, like the first, bears no relation to the experiences of the vast majority of my 50 women. Far from existing in isolation, most of these women have created lives of sustained intimacy. No doubt, Gubrium correctly described the experiences of the single elders he studied; yet—to repeat a conclusion stated earlier—the subculture of old, never-married women is peopled with socially active *and* socially isolated members. *Both* must be understood in order to penetrate the complexity and variation of single life in old age in the United States.

Among scholars who study the elderly, four theories concerning the aging process have seized the lion's share of attention: (1) disengagement, (2) activity, (3) continuity, and (4) age stratificati
The first two theories are at odds with the old-age experi
recounted by the 50 never-married women with whom I
However, the second two theories, by contrast, resonate
information and interpretations that these 50 actors voll

The disengagement theory, first articulated by Elain
and William Henry, posits inevitable withdrawal fro
old people, sought by society and the elderly alike. C
argued, pull back from social interactions and cu
order to free themselves from external pressure
opportunities for reflection. Society, at the sar
from old people in order to make room for y
mize the social disruption resulting from d
efficiency among its most active participar

In attempting to apply the disengage
of old, never-married women, two pro'
duction in activity and relationships '
study (16 of 50) was involuntary. Si
erty, and mandatory retirement cc

forces of disengagement, *not* growing "interiority or diminishing ego involvement."[11] Indeed, none of the never-married women I interviewed wanted to reduce their involvement in relationships, organizations, or activities after retiring. Instead, their "withdrawal" (by 32 percent of the women) from some portions of social life is far better explained by James Dowd's exchange theory than by disengagement theory.

Dowd highlights the power dependency of the old. He conceptualizes aging as a process of social exchange in which "the partner . . . who is less dependent on that exchange enjoys a power advantage. Such an advantage can then be utilized to effect compliance from the exchange partner." Society and its institutions are one partner of the social exchange; an old person is the other partner. Since society is less dependent for resources and power on an individual who is old than vice versa, it and its subdivisions (such as the labor market, government, or the health care system) are in a position to exclude a never-married old woman from full involvement and to penalize her financially, thus forcing further disengagement.[12]

A second reason for rejecting the disengagement theory is that most of the women I interviewed gave no evidence of either quantitative or qualitative withdrawal from the affairs and routines of everyday life. Despite their loss of full-time employment, 34 of the women detailed a wide variety of social contacts and activities that matched or (in a few cases) exceeded their level of engagement before retirement. Through family connections, friendships, neighbors, church or synagogue, part-time work, travel, volunteer activities, and political involvement, most of these women were as active and sustained as rich a network of contacts, as they had throughout adulthood. For example:

I retired early so that I would have plenty of time to do those things I could not do while I was caring for Papa

and holding down a nine-to-five job. What are those things I do now that I didn't do before sixty? Travel, lots and lots of it. I don't have any money to speak of, but when I get wanderlust, I just sell some pieces of furniture from the house or some pieces of jewelry that Mama left me. Or I take a bit of bookkeeping on the side (and under the table).

When I am not traveling, I work with blind kids a day a week and read those books that have been on my "must read" list for years. I also put one day a week into tutoring in an adult literacy project that our church undertook. Then, every Thursday afternoon and evening that I am in town, I take an intensive conversational Spanish course. I do that because I head up our church's work with refugees from Central America. I want to be able to talk with the people we give refuge to. Then, too, I see a lot of my friends, but then that has always been so. Sometimes, my body makes me slow down some. But only a wee bit, I can assure you. [July 1983]

Activity theory, like disengagement theory, also bears little relation to the ages of the women I interviewed. Activity theorists, such as Robert Havighurst, hold that "successful aging" requires that older people maintain the attitudes and activities of middle age for as many years as possible and that they replace former work and social roles with new activities.[13] Satisfactory old age, according to this theory, is accomplished by making the retirement years as much like middle age as possible.

Not one of these 50 women understood her commitments and relationships in old age to be substitutive. Instead, they all viewed their activities and friendships after retirement as uninterrupted continuations of long-standing habits and priorities, or as new responses to lifelong needs and predispositions. One woman expressed the group's disinterest in "privileging" or preserving their middle-aged habits, as well as their interest in fashioning an old age that sustains old relationships and explores fresh ones:

> Sixty-five couldn't come fast enough, as far as I was concerned, for then I could retire with full benefits and begin to live as I had long wished to—spending lots of time with old friends, working in my garden, and learning Swedish.
>
> By age sixty-eight, I had mastered Swedish thoroughly. So I was then able to carry out a dream I had cherished since I was a young girl—to go back to live in the village from which both my grandmother and grandfather had emigrated in the 1880s. From my sixty-eighth to my seventy-fourth year I lived in Timburgen. It was glorious. I eventually came back here because I missed my friends terribly. But what an adventure it was to go backwards and forwards at the same time. [March 1984]

Old age, for this woman, was an opportunity to honor her grandparents and to investigate, at firsthand, their homeland, which had intrigued her since childhood.

Continuity theory, as conceptualized by Robert Atchley, posits the merging of past with present, which these women achieved in old age:

> The *continuity* or consolidation approach to individual aging assumes that, in the process of becoming adults,

individuals develop habits, commitments, preferences, and a host of other dispositions that become a part of their personalities. As individuals grow older, they are predisposed toward maintaining continuity. They cope with activity losses by consolidating their activities and redistributing their commitments among those activities that remain. The continuity approach does *not* assume that lost roles need be replaced.

In this context, *continuity* means that the individual's reaction to aging can be explained by examining the complex interrelationships among biological and psychological changes; the person's habits, preferences, and associations; situational opportunities for continuity; and actual experience. Lifelong experience thus creates certain predispositions that individuals will maintain if at all possible. . . . At all phases of the life course, these predispositions constantly evolve from interactions among personal preferences, biological and psychological capabilities, situational opportunities, and experience. Adaptation is a process involving interaction among all of these elements.[14]

The women's quests for continuity in retirement have resulted, in 31 of the 50 cases, in an adventurous approach to old age. Those women who demonstrated an exploratory spirit as youths or young adults in their social relationships, worklives, or community or religious activities have replicated that attitude and behavior in their old age. Once the responsibility of caring for aging parents and of earning a living was removed, these 31 women began projects and relationships in their sixties, seventies, eighties, and nineties that "stretched" their vision and capacities. Some traveled widely, despite limited funds. Others initiated community projects, such as a hotline for shut-in elderly people, a parish soup kitchen for the homeless, a study group in liberation theology for aging Puerto Rican women, and a shelter for runaway youths. Still others experimented in cultural realms: learning foreign languages or computer skills, writing articles or books, taking up painting, a musical instrument, or modern dancing. Three women became clients in psychotherapy, hoping to find more pleasure and self-esteem in old age than they had in middle age. After retiring, 4 retrained in a new trade or profession. Thirty-one of the women, in sum, have renewed their adventurousness as retirees. They have shaped a coda that recapitulates the motifs of their earlier years, in which they chose to remain single, while more than 9 out of 10 of their "sisters" married.

The words of one of these women express the continuity of her risk taking, which had been disrupted in her fifties by the responsibilities of care-giving:

> Mama was critically ill for two and a half years. When she passed on, I was at a great loss for about six months. Then I got the bright idea to retire as soon as I could draw a full pension.
>
> One month after retiring, I became a lay worker with the Sisters of Charity. I volunteered for duty in a mission in Indochina. I worked with lepers there until three years ago, using the many years of nursing that I had under my belt. In my high school years, I had dreamed of such a mission. Those were the years in which I volunteered in a settlement house on the sly, defying my mother, who had explicitly forbidden me to do that. When she found out about that, I was seventeen. She threw me out of her house for six or seven years, until we finally came to terms. [September 1983]

Another woman's comments also reveal the sense of adventure with which retirement was viewed:

> The piano and flute had been my instruments since public school days. But then, when I retired, my days appeared to me as chances to study clarinet, violin, and electric bass. That last sounds a bit ridiculous, I know, for an old lady. But such interesting music is being written now for the bass.
>
> Before I get really old, I am going to study conducting. That dream used to sustain me in some of my secretarial jobs that bored me silly. I used to fantasize being in front of a great orchestra while I typed away. Last year, I applied for conducting apprenticeships here in the city. There are several good ones and one superb one. One of them would have nothing to do with me. Two others told me that if I took several more music theory classes, I would be seriously reconsidered in 1984–1985. Who knows if they were being truthful with me? Of course, I will move forward as if they meant what they said. [May 1984]

The women I interviewed—both the group of 31 for whom old age was a continued pursuit of innovation and the set of 19 for whom retirement meant, primarily, deeper commitments to old friends and familiar activities—have interpreted their postretirement lives from at least two perspectives. They are conscious of their respective generations and are, at the same time, individuals with idiosyncratic inclinations. At the time of the interviews, they demonstrated full awareness of "age stratification," Matilda Riley's term for the unique socialization each birth cohort undergoes and the shared construction of reality that each generation develops in the course of living within a given chronology in history. The sociology of aging, Riley argues, is an "interplay between two dynamisms: social change and the process of aging."[15] The nature of old age for any individual, in other words, is a function of three interactive forces: (1) the historical and sociological changes and trends during a person's childhood, adulthood, and old age; (2) the physiological, social, and psychological process of an individual's moving through life; and (3) the consciousness and experiences shared by a generation of individuals born in the same era and raised under similar historical conditions.

Many of the women talked about the conjunction of their young adulthood, middle age, or old age with particular social or cultural upheavals of the twentieth century. As a group, they were acutely aware of the "placement of their biographies" within an historical chronology. They spoke often of the common ground they shared with those who were born at the turn of the century or in the "Progressive Era." One woman said:

> I was born in 1912, year of the Bull Moosers, a time of solemn hope for reformers. What an optimistic time that was, my parents used to tell me.
>
> But things turned sour as I left childhood behind. I was seventeen when the market crashed, just graduating from high school. Everybody I knew in my high school class, including me, grabbed at any job they could get and held on to it for dear life.
>
> I released my death grip on that first job as soon as the war brought us some relief. I was just reaching my thirties when the war began and felt genuine optimism, believe it or not, at the prospect of the war's build-up. It took me years to admit that to myself, since we are supposed to hate war. But for me, at age thirty, the war meant a welcome change.   [November 1982]

Another woman reflected on the happy intersection of her old age with the "Gray Power" movement:

> It matters enormously that I got old when I did. I am *not* a particularly political creature. But all the same I benefit a lot from the political ruckus raised by those Gray Power people.
>
> I retired in 1976. By that time, you could get free bus passes, low-cost movie tickets, and apologies if someone insults your old age. The most important premium I get for being old at this time is that I get listened to in places that are afraid of lawsuits. If, for example, employees overlook me in stores or offices, I rattle their cage a bit when I say: "I demand some attention. You can't treat old people this way unless you want to end up in court!"   [January 1984]

Other women put greater emphasis on the coincidence of their late middle age or old age with the second phase of the U.S. women's movement. Without exception, the 7 women who broached this topic said their retirement years had been enhanced by the growing awareness of sexism and of women's special needs and contributions. Another woman, who characterized herself as "alien to politics," said:

> I was the first on my block to condemn those "libbers." They seemed to me to be a bunch of whiners—people who would rather complain than get on with a day's work.
>
> Then one morning I was watching the Phil Donahue show. He had on experts on women's health care. That hour I learned encyclopedias full about pregnancy and

menopause and bone diseases that affect women in particular in their later years.

That week I went to a clinic and got my bones checked. Sure enough, I had some problems with calcium deficiency. The doctors told me that I had come in early enough to forestall the worst sort of consequences that come from insufficient calcium. I took huge amounts of calcium supplements for awhile and exercised my legs and body in the ways recommended to me. As a result, my bone problems are minor ones now. Had it not been for those "libbers" who got interested in the special concerns of old women, Donahue would never have reported on something that could, the doctors say, have cost me the ability to walk.   [June 1983]

Her comments were the most dramatic expressions uttered by these women on the impact of the women's movement on their old age. Yet, like the woman above, 6 others described feminism as a force which spotlighted and legitimated women's problems and issues that had previously gone unnoticed.

Repeatedly, the women communicated their sense of themselves as members of a generation cursed by the Depression in the prime of their adulthood, but blessed by the opportunities that accompanied wartime, and by the political leavening of the 1960s and 1970s as well. To a great degree, they "identified" with others of their age group who had negotiated the twentieth century at the same time. Their feelings of generational solidarity penetrated the interviews at many points, revealing their finely tuned historical and sociological sensibilities.

The narratives of these never-married women underscore at least two fundamental kinds of imbalance: (1) the inequities in the division of labor between men and women within families and

(2) the lopsided responsibility between the state and the family in care for the dependent elderly. The first imbalance appeared again and again in remembrances of siblings' decision-making as to who would care for aged or dying family members and who would maintain the family household, once parents were no longer willing or able to do so. These women frequently took or were given by default, responsibility for both. Seemingly, their gender, as well as their marital status, "preordained" such assignments. Though most of the women who took on family care-giving and housekeeping did not resent performing these services and functions, most of them expressed bitterness over the "unavailability" of siblings—brothers in particular—for sharing such tasks. The lives of never-married women would be much improved if siblings of both genders, whether married or unmarried, took their fair shares of care-giving responsibility. Such a notion of familial fairness is, of course, a pipe dream, without a massive reworking of gender-role socialization and of the educational system, as well as of the labor market's treatment of women and men.

To examine reallocation of responsibility for dependent aged within families, without examining the state's accountability for old people, is to minimize the government's responsibility in sustaining and caring for dependent citizens. Those who work to dismantle the welfare state would do so by expanding the "family's" (that is, women's) already huge share in providing for members and relatives who are too young, too sick, too immobile, or too disabled to care for themselves. As gerontologist Alan Walker has noted:

> The current social division of caring roles and responsibilities is not is the interest of either women or elderly people. The "community care" of the elderly relies on women forfeiting other activities, including careers, and

being subjected to considerable physical and emotional stress. Elderly people share the effects of this stress on women and the family and when the principal carer can bear the strain no longer the elderly person is likely to end up in a residential institution. . . .

Policies framed on the assumption that the role of the state should continue to be confined to crisis intervention and the family should be the main provider of care to the elderly suffer from two fundamental deficiencies. First of all, they reinforce the unequal division of caring between the sexes, and while one person shoulders the whole responsibility for caring, this role and the dependency relationship associated with it will continue to engender stress and fatigue. Secondly, they further reduce the independence of elderly people and their interdependencies within the family and wider community.[16]

The state must institute policies drastically different from those that now prevail if we are to assure old people of quality care and of maximal autonomy. As sociologist Beth Hess has stressed, a progressive social policy that is responsive both to old people and their care-giving relatives, friends, and neighbors would:

First of all focus on maintaining old people in their own residences for as long as possible while also providing a spectrum of community-based services to relieve the burdens on caregiving kin: Visiting nurses and homemakers, meal delivery, an adult day-care center, transportation assistance, and respite services—in fact, all the programs that are currently losing their funding or being folded into block grants to be fought over at the state level.[17]

In addition, a policy of supporting old people in their own homes would require implementation of health-care financing programs already in place in parts of Western Europe. An "attendance allowance" would enable the dependent elderly to purchase both domestic and nursing care. An "invalid allowance," available to all care-givers, regardless of gender and marital status, who attend partially or totally disabled persons, would pay for services now delivered by unpaid wives, daughters, relatives, friends, lovers, or neighbors at great cost to their jobs, pay, relationships, energy, time, and well-being.[18]

Furthermore, housing costs for the elderly must be addressed by the state if old people are to stay in their houses or apartments and thereby avoid unnecessary institutionalization. Subsidized rental housing and rent control are needed to provide reasonably priced houses and apartments to old people on limited and fixed incomes. However, federal programs for constructing low-cost housing have been slashed since 1981, and federal programs for subsidizing rents in existing housing are unavailable for most older Americans.[19] Local rent stabilization and rent control laws, where they exist, are opposed by well-financed property developers and landlords.

The accounts of these never-married women also call into serious question mandatory retirement laws and regulations, which have clearly taken a toll—economic, social, and psychological—on them. One can speculate that the employers of these seasoned workers also paid a high price, in lost expertise and loyalty, from forced retirements. If mandatory retirement is outlawed, workers, unions, and employers would be much freer to establish, on a worker-by-worker basis, the best partial and full retirement plans. More broadly, old workers are entitled to full employment, education, and job training.

With little money yet ample resources, these 50 never-married women have negotiated single life in their old age with adaptive aplomb. In part, their relative well-being in retirement rests on their self-reliance. As never-married women, they entered retirement with many decades of practice in providing for their own welfare, despite severely limited funds.

Self-reliance, however, is only one element of their success in enjoying old age and contending with its difficulties. Of equal importance to their welfare after the age of sixty-five is their well-developed capacity to rely to some extent on others, on friends and family. Through many years of single life, these women have discerned both the value and the limitations of independence. Long before retirement, each woman devised her own particular blend of autonomy and dependence. This mix has proved to be invaluable in the last third of her single life.

Notes

ONE

1. William Wordsworth, "Personal Talk," in Alice N. George, ed., *The Complete Poetical Works of Wordsworth* (Boston: Houghton Mifflin, 1932; orig. pub. 1806–7), pp. 346–347; William Blake, "Proverbs of Hell in the Marriage of Heaven and Hell," in Geoffrey Keynes, ed., *The Complete Writings of William Blake* (London: Oxford University Press, 1966; orig. pub. 1790–93), pp. 150–151; Alexander Pope, "January and May: or the Merchant's Tale," in H. W. Boynton, ed., *The Complete Poetical Works of Pope* (Boston: Houghton Mifflin, 1931; orig. pub. 1709), pp. 35–46.

2. William Faulkner, *The Sound and the Fury* (New York: Random House, 1929), p. 167.

3. In Rosabeth M. Kanter, *Men and Women of the Corporation* (New York: Basic Books, 1977), p. 201.

4. Sunoco advertisement, Veterans Stadium scoreboard, Philadelphia, July 12, 1983.

5. Lee Chambers-Schiller, *Liberty, a Better Husband: Single Women in America: The Generations of 1780–1840.* (New Haven: Yale University Press, 1984), p. 18.

6. William R. Greer, "The Changing Women's Marriage Market," *New York Times*, February 22, 1986, p. 48. This article reports on a study by Neil Bennett, Patricia Craig, and David Bloom, who made demographic projections, based on parametric modeling techniques, applied to U.S. Census data gathered from 70,000 households in 1982.

7. "The New Look in Old Maids," *People*, March 31, 1986, pp. 28–33.

8. Laurel Richardson, *The New Other Woman: Single Women in Affairs with Married Men* (New York: Free Press, 1985), pp. 2–4.

9. Greer, "Changing Women's Marriage Market," p. 48.

10. Clifford Geertz, *The Interpretation of Cultures* (New York: Basic Books, 1973), p. 5.

11. Peter J. Stein, *Single Life: Unmarried Adults in Social Context* (New York: St. Martin's Press, 1981), pp. 17–18.

12. Ibid., p. 9.

13. Jacqueline Jones, *Labor of Love, Labor of Sorrow: Black Women, Work, and the Family from Slavery to the Present* (New York: Basic Books, 1985), p. 154.

14. Elizabeth Higginbotham, "Is Marriage a Priority? Class Differences in Marital Options of Educated Black Women," in Stein, ed., *Single Life*, pp. 259–267.

15. Robert Staples, *The World of Black Singles* (Westport, Conn.: Greenwood Press, 1981), p. 11.

16. Everett Hughes, "Dilemmas and Contradictions of Status," *American Journal of Sociology* 50 (1945): 353–359.

17. Mary Douglas, *Purity and Danger: An Analysis of Pollution and Taboo* (Boston: Routledge & Kegan Paul, 1966), pp. 98–99.

18. Ibid., p. 102

19. Michelle Fine and Adienne Asch, "Disabled Women: Sexism without the Pedestal," *Journal of Sociology and Social Welfare* 8 (1981): 233–240.

20. Ibid., p. 240.

21. Erving Goffman, *Stigma: Notes on the Management of Spoiled Identity* (Englewood Cliffs, N.J.: Prentice-Hall, 1963), pp. 1–5.

22. Ibid., p. 10.

23. Clara Mayo, "Training for Positive Marginality," in *Applied Social Psychology Annual* (Beverly Hills, Calif.: Sage, 1982), pp. 55–73.

24. Sarah H. Matthews, *The Social World of Old Women: Management of Self Identity* (Beverly Hills, Calif.: Sage, 1979), p. 151.

25. Ibid., pp. 19–20.

26. Lee Chambers-Schiller, "The Single Woman Reformer: Conflicts Between Family and Vocation, 1830–1860," *Frontiers* 3 (1978): 41–48.

27. Ibid., p. 41.

28. Suzanne Gordon, *Lonely in America* (New York: Simon & Schuster, 1976), p. 83.

29. Lillian Faderman, *Surpassing the Love of Men* (New York: Morrow, 1981), p. 241.

30. Daniel S. Smith, "Family Limitation, Sexual Control, and Domestic Feminism in Victorian America," in Mary Hartman and Lois Banner, eds., *Clio's Consciousness Raised* (New York: Harper Torchbooks, 1974), pp. 119–136.

31. Lee Chambers-Schiller, *Liberty*, p. 3.

32. Smith, "Family Limitations," p. 121.

33. Ibid.

34. U.S. Bureau of the Census, *Marital Status and Living Arrangements: March 1979*, Current Population Reports, Series P-20, No. 349 (Washington, D.C.: U.S. Government Printing Office, 1980), p. 2.

35. U.S. Bureau of the Census, *1980 Census of Population*, Vol. 1, *Characteristics of the Population*, Chap. D, "Detailed Population Characteristics," Part 1, Sec. A (Washington, D.C.: U.S. Government Printing Office, 1984), Table 253, pp. 1–7; *Statistical Abstract of the United States: 1986*, 106th ed. (Washington, D.C.: U.S. Government Printing Office, 1985), pp. 31–41.

36. Sara E. Rix, *Older Women: The Economics of Aging* (Washington, D.C.: Women's Research and Education Institute of the Congressional Caucus for Women's Issues, 1984), Table 10, p. 19.

37. Ibid., p. 19.

38. U.S. Bureau of the Census, *Current Population Reports*, Series P-20, No. 347 (Washington, D.C.: U.S. Government Printing Office, 1981), Table 6–3, p. 37.

39. Rita Braito and Donna Anderson, "The Ever-Single Elderly Woman," in Elizabeth W. Markson, ed., *Older Women: Issues and Prospects* (Lexington, Mass.: Lexington Books, 1983), pp. 195–225.

40. U.S. Bureau of the Census, *Current Population Reports*, Series P-20, No. 412 (Washington, D.C.: U.S. Government Printing Office, 1984), Table 62, p. 21.

41. Ibid.

42. U.S. Bureau of the Census, *1980 Census of Population*, Table 253, pp. 1–7.

43. U.S. Bureau of the Census, *Statistical Abstract of the United States: 1984*, 104th ed. (Washington, D.C.: U.S. Government Printing Office, 1983), p. 18.

44. U.S. Bureau of the Census, *1980 Census of Population*, Table 253, pp. 1–7.

45. U.S. Bureau of the Census, *Statistical Abstract of the United States: 1986*, p. 36; Lois M. Verbrugge, "Marital Status and Health," *Journal of Marriage and the Family* 41 (1979): 267–285.

46. Lois Verbrugge, "Marital Status and Health," p. 282.

TWO

1. Susan B. Anthony, "Homes of Single Women," in Ellen C. Dubois, ed., *Elizabeth Cady Stanton: Correspondence, Writings, Speeches* (New York: Schocken, 1981), pp. 146–151.

2. Clifford Geertz, *Local Knowledge: Further Essays in Interpretive Anthropology* (New York: Basic Books, 1983), p. 58.

3. Ibid., pp. 57–58, 58.

4. Anthony, "Homes of Single Women," p. 148.

5. Martha B. Vicinus, *Independent Women: Work and Community for Single Women, 1850–1920* (Chicago: University of Chicago Press, 1985), pp. 292, 291.

6. Jane Austen, *Emma*, in *The Complete Novels of Jane Austen* (New York: Random House, 1959; orig. pub. 1816), pp. 763–1060.

7. Peter J. Stein, *Single Life: Unmarried Adults in Social Contexts* (New York: St. Martin's, 1981), pp. 10–11.

8. Edward P. Thompson, *The Making of the English Working Class* (New York: Vintage, 1963), p. 12.

9. Robert Staples, "Black Singles in America," in Peter J. Stein, ed., *Single Life* (New York: St. Martin's Press, 1981), pp. 40–51.

10. This reference to the desirability of sustaining the independence of girlhood is reminiscent of Catherine Beecher's outlook as a single adult in a much earlier era. Beecher, a prominent American educator, who was born in 1800, experienced contradictions between the passive dependency "her father and culture" expected of her as an adult woman and the assertive initiative her father, evangelist Lyman Beecher, had encouraged in her as a child. One way Beecher found to alleviate this contradiction was to avoid becoming a wife, a role that she feared might subsume her individu-

ality as her mother's had been subsumed in her father's household. Instead, she set up her own household and actively pursued a career. See Kathryn K. Sklar, *Catherine Beecher: A Study in American Domesticity* (New Haven: Yale University Press, 1973), pp. 54, 31–32.

11. Vicinus, *Independent Women*, p. 5.

12. See Rosalind Rosenburg, *Beyond Separate Spheres: Intellectual Roots of Modern Feminism* (New Haven: Yale University Press, 1982).

13. Robert Bellah, Richard Madsen, William M. Sullivan, Ann Swidler, and Steven M. Tipton, *Habits of the Heart: Individualism and Commitment in American Life* (Berkeley: University of California Press, 1985), p. 66.

14. Carmel Dinan, "Pragmatism or Feminists? The Professional "Single" Women of Accra, Ghana," *Cahiers d'études africaines* 17 (1977): 155–176, 174.

15. Matilda W. Riley, "Social Gerontology and the Age of Stratification of Society," in C. S. Kart and B. B. Barnard, eds., *Aging in America: Readings in Social Gerontology* (Sherman Oaks, Calif.: Alfred Publishing Co., 1981), pp. 133–149.

16. Karl Mannheim, "The Problem of Generations," in P. Kecskemeti, ed., *Essays on the Sociology of Knowledge* (New York: Oxford University Press, 1952), pp. 276–290.

THREE

1. Alan G. Davis and Philip M. Strong, "Working Without a Net: the Bachelor as a Social Problem," *Sociological Review* 25 (1977): 109–129.

2. See Christopher Lasch, *Haven in a Heartless World: The Family Beseiged* (New York: Basic Books, 1979).

3. Harriette P. McAdoo, "Black Mothers and the Extended Support Network," in L. F. Rodgers-Rose, ed., *The Black Woman* (Beverly Hills, Calif.: Sage, 1980), pp. 125–144.

4. See Ian A. Canino and Glorisa Canino, "Impact of Stress on the Puerto Rican Family: Treatment Considerations," *American Journal of Orthopsychiatry* 50 (1980): 535–541. These 4 women's descriptions of family life conformed closely to the pattern of "normal enmeshment" that the Caninos have found to be characteristic of Puerto Rican American families.

5. See John G. Red Horse, "American Indian Elders: Unifiers of Indian Families," *Social Casework* 61 (1980): 490–493; and John G. Red Horse, "Family Structure and Value Orientation in American Indians," ibid., pp. 462–467.

6. Patricia A. Palmieri, "Patterns of Achievement of Single Academic Women at Wellesley College, 1880–1920," *Frontiers* 5 (1980): 63–67.

7. See Elaine M. Brody, "Women in the Middle and Family Help to Older People," *Gerontologist* 21 (1981): 471–480; Elinor Polansky, "Women and the Health Care System: Implications for Social Work Practice," in Elaine Norman and Arlene Mancuso, eds., *Women's Issues and Social Work Practice* (Itasca, Ill.: Peacock, 1980), pp. 83–199; Janet Finch and Dulcie Groves, eds., *A Labour of Love: Women, Work and Caring* (Boston: Routledge & Kegan Paul, 1983).

8. Davis and Strong, "Working Without a Net," p. 122.

9. Glen H. Elder and Jeffrey K. Liker, "Hard Times in Women's Lives: Historical Influences across Forty Years," *American Journal of Sociology* 88 (1982): 241–269.

10. Jane Addams, "The Subjective Necessity for Social Settlements," in Christopher Lasch, ed., *The Social Thought of Jane Addams* (New York: Bobbs-Merril, 1965; orig. pub. 1892), pp. 28–43.

FOUR

1. Robert Paine, "In Search of Friendship: An Exploratory Analysis in Middle-Class Culture," *Man* 4 (1969): 505–524.

2. Michele Barrett and Mary McIntosh, *The Anti-Social Family* (New York: Schocken, 1982), p. 80.

3. Rita Braito and Donna Anderson, "The Ever-Single Elderly Woman," in Elizabeth Markson, ed., *Older Women: Issues and Prospects* (Lexington, Mass.: Lexington Books, 1983), pp. 195–225.

4. Georg Simmel, "The Isolated Individual and the Dyad," in F. H. Wolff, ed., *The Sociology of Georg Simmel* (New York: Free Press, 1950; orig. pub. 1908), pp. 118–144.

5. George Levinger and Harold Raush, *Close Relationships: Perspectives on the Meaning of Intimacy* (Amherst: University of Massachusetts Press, 1977), pp. 1–11, 137–161.

6. Robert Bell, *Worlds of Friendship* (Beverly Hills, Calif.: Sage, 1981), p. 19.

7. For background on same-sex friendships in Victorian America, see Carroll Smith-Rosenberg, "The Female World of Love and Ritual: Relations Between Women in Nineteenth-Century America," *Signs: Journal of Women in Culture and Society* 1 (1975): 1–29.

8. U.S. Bureau of the Census, *Marital Status and Living Arrangements: March 1983*, Current Population Reports, Series P-20, No. 389 (Washington, D.C.: U.S. Government Printing Office, 1984), Table B, p. 2.

9. Lillian Faderman, *Surpassing the Love of Men* (New York: Morrow, 1981), pp. 238–248.

10. Nancy Cott, "Passionlessness: An Interpretation of Victorian Sexual Ideology, 1790–1850," *Signs* 4 (1978): 219–236.

11. Carroll Smith-Rosenberg, "History of Lesbianism," lecture at the Annenberg School of Communication, University of Pennsylvania, Philadelphia, May 9, 1983.

12. Michel Foucault, *The History of Sexuality*, vol. 1 (New York: Pantheon, 1978), pp. 17–26.

13. Beth Hess, "Friendship," in Matilda W. Riley, ed., *Aging and Society*, vol. 3: *A Sociology of Age Stratification* (New York: Russell Sage Foundation, 1972), pp. 357–393.

14. Robert Weiss, "The Study of Loneliness," in P. J. Stein, ed., *Single Life: Unmarried Adults in Social Contexts* (New York: St. Martin's Press, 1981), pp. 152–164.

15. Martha A. Ackelsberg, "Sisters or Comrades? The Politics of Friends and Families," in I. Diamond, ed., *Families, Politics, and Public Policy: A Feminist Dialogue on Women and the State* (New York: Longman, 1983), pp. 339–365.

16. Adrienne Rich, "Compulsory Heterosexuality and Lesbian Existence," *Signs* 5 (1980): 631–660. See also Ann Ferguson, Jacquelyn Zita, and Kathryn P. Addelson, "On Compulsory Heterosexuality and Lesbian Existence: Defining the Issues," *Signs* 7 (1981): 158–199.

FIVE

1. U.S. Department of Labor, Employment Standards Administration, Women's Bureau, *Handbook on Women Workers*, Bulletin No. 297 (Washington, D.C.: U.S. Government Printing Office, 1975), Table 57, p. 136; *Handbook on Women Workers*, Bulletin No. 294, 1969, Table 61,

p. 137; *Handbook on Women Workers* Bulletin No. 261, 1956, Table 10, p. 44; *Handbook of Facts on Women Workers*, Bulletin No. 225, 1948, Table 5, p. 22; and U.S. Bureau of the Census, *Money Income of Household, Families and Persons in the U.S.: 1982*, Current Population Reports, Series P-60, No. 142 (Washington, D.C.: U.S. Government Printing Office, 1984), Table 37, pp. 117–118; U.S. Bureau of the Census, *Statistical Abstract of the United States: 1986*, 106th ed. (Washington, D.C.: U.S. Government Printing Office, 1985), Table 704, p. 419.

2. U.S. Department of Labor, Women's Bureau, *The Earnings Gap Between Women and Men* (Washington, D.C.: U.S. Government Printing Office, 1979), Table 1, p. 6.

3. Twentieth Century Fund Task Force on Women and Employment, *Exploitation from 9 to 5* (Lexington, Mass.: Lexington Books, 1975), p. 50.

4. Alice Kessler-Harris, *Out to Work: A History of Wage-Earning Women in the United States* (New York: Oxford University Press, 1982), p. 249.

5. Twentieth Century Fund, *Exploitation from 9 to 5*, p. 50.

6. Ibid.

7. Patricia Roos, *Gender and Work: A Comparative Analysis of Industrial Societies* (Albany: State University of New York Press, 1985), pp. 51–52, 66.

8. Jacqueline Jones, *Labor of Love, Labor of Sorrow: Black Women, Work, and the Family from Slavery to the Present* (New York: Basic Books, 1985), p. 199.

9. Ibid., pp. 166, 200, 234–235.

10. Roos, *Gender and Work*, pp. 135, 153.

11. Ibid., p. 154.

12. Claudia Goldin, "The Work and Wages of Single Women, 1870–1920," *Journal of Economic History* 40 (1980): 81–88.

13. Martha B. Vicinus, *Independent Women: Work and Community for Single Women, 1850–1920* (Chicago: University of Chicago Press, 1985), p. 6.

14. Lewis Coser, *Greedy Institutions: Patterns of Unidivided Commitment* (New York: Free Press, 1974), pp. 4–6.

15. See Alan Davis and Philip Strong, "Working Without a Net: The Bachelor as a Social Problem," *Sociological Review* 25 (1977): 109–129.

16. Valerie K. Oppenheimer, *The Female Labor Force in the United States* (Berkeley: University of California Press, 1970), p. 130.

17. Kessler-Harris, *Out to Work*, p. 235.

18. Susan Ware, *Holding Their Own: American Women in the 1930s* (Boston: Twayne, 1982), p. 28.

19. In a conversation in New York City in 1985.

20. Kessler-Harris, *Out to Work*, p. 261.

21. Ruth Milkman, "Women's Work and Economic Crisis: Some Lessons of the Great Depression," *Review of Radical Political Economics* 8 (1976): 81–85.

22. Ware, *Holding Their Own*, pp. 21–35; Kessler-Harris, *Out to Work*, pp. 235–295.

23. U.S. Bureau of the Census, *Historical Statistics of the U.S.— Colonial Times to 1970*, Part I, Series D 85–86 (Washington, D.C.: U.S. Government Printing Office, 1975), p. 135.

24. See Peter Marris, *Loss and Change* (New York: Pantheon, 1974), pp. 1–22.

25. Kessler-Harris, *Out to Work*, p. 295.

26. Jones, *Labor of Love*. p. 236.

SIX

1. Bureau of the Census, *Statistical Abstract of the United States: 1985*, 105th ed. (Washington, D.C.: U.S. Government Printing Office, 1985), Table 736, p. 443.

2. Ibid., Table 760, p. 456.

3. Ibid., p. 429.

4. See Sara E. Rix, *Older Women: The Economics of Aging* (Washington, D.C.: Women's Research and Education Institute of the Congressional Caucus for Women's Issues, 1984), p. 9.

5. Ibid., Table 8, p. 15.

6. U.S. Bureau of the Census, *Current Population Reports*, Series P-20, No. 389 (Washington, D.C.: U.S. Government Printing Office, 1984), Table 1.

7. Irving Rosow, *Socialization to Old Age* (Berkeley: University of California Press, 1974), pp. 88–91.

8. Arlie Russell Hochschild, *The Unexpected Community: Portrait of an Old Age Subculture*, 3rd ed. (Berkeley: University of California Press, 1983).

9. Jaber F. Gubrium, "Being Single in Old Age," in J. F. Gubrium, ed., *Time, Roles and Self in Old Age* (New York: Human Sciences Press, 1976), pp. 179–195.

10. Elaine Cumming and William Henry, *Growing Old: The Process of Disengagement* (New York: Basic Books, 1961).

11. Harold Cox, *Later Life: The Realities of Aging* (Englewood Cliffs, N.J.: Prentice-Hall, 1984), p. 000.

12. See James J. Dowd, "Aging as Exchange: A Preface to Theory," *Journal of Gerontology* 30 (1975): 584–594, and James J. Dowd, and Ralph LaRossa, "Primary Group and Elderly Morale: An Exchange/Power Analysis," *Sociology and Social Research* 66 (1982): 184–197.

13. Robert J. Havighurst, "Disengagement and Patterns of Aging" in Bernice L. Neugarten, ed., *Middle Age and Aging* (Chicago: University of Chicago Press, 1968), pp. 161–172.

14. Robert C. Atchley, *The Social Forces in Later Life: An Introduction to Social Gerontology* (Belmont, Calif.: Wadsworth, 1972).

15. Matilda W. Riley, Marilyn Johnson, and Anne Foner, eds., *Aging and Society*, vol. 3: *A Sociology of Age Stratification* (New York: Russell Sage Foundation, 1972), and Matilda W. Riley, "Aging, Social Change, and the Power of Ideas," *Daedalus* 107 (1978): 39–52.

16. Alan Walker, "Care for Elderly People: A Conflict Between Women and the State" in Janet Finch and Dulcie Groves, eds., *A Labour of Love: Women, Work, and Caring* (London: Routledge & Kegan Paul, 1983), pp. 106–128.

17. Beth B. Hess, "Aging Policies and Old Women: The Hidden Agenda," in A. Rossi, ed., *Gender and the Life Course* (Chicago: Aldine, 1985), pp. 319–331.

18. See Dulcie Groves and Janet Finch, "Natural Selection: Perspectives on Entitlement to the Invalid Care Allowance," in Finch and Groves, eds., *A Labour of Love*, pp. 148–166.

19. Hess, "Aging Policies and Old Women," pp. 319–331.

Index